FULL STEAM AHEAD

For the Railways of London & the South East 2010-2011

EDITOR
John Robinson

First Edition

RAILWAY LOCATOR MAP

The numbers shown on this map relate to the page numbers for each railway.
Pages 5-6 contain an alphabetical listing of the railways featured in this guide.
Please note that the markers on this map show the approximate location only.

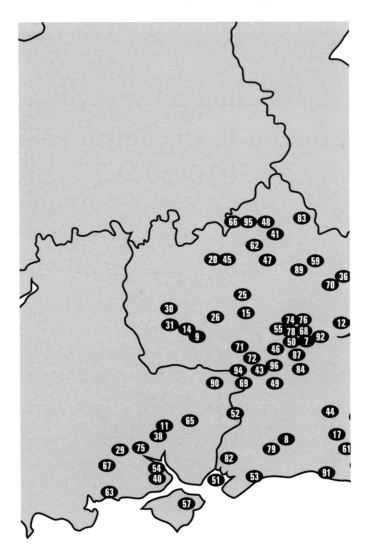

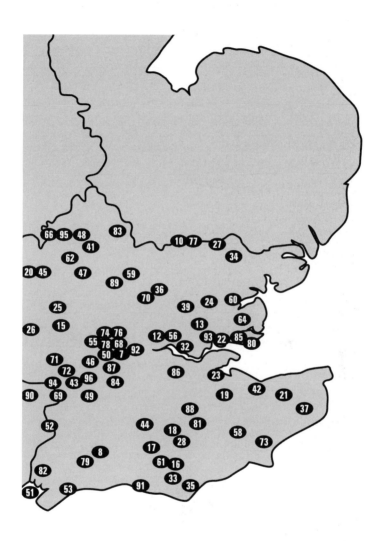

ACKNOWLEDGEMENTS

We were greatly impressed by the friendly and cooperative manner of the staff and helpers of the railways and societies which we selected to appear in this book, and wish to thank them all for the help they have given. In addition we wish to thank Bob Budd (cover design) and Michael Robinson (page layouts) for their help. Also Lionel Parker and members of the Frimley and Ascot Locomotive Club for providing two of the photographs used on the cover.

We are particularly indebted to Peter Bryant for his invaluable assistance. Peter's web site: www.miniaturerailwayworld.co.uk provides a great deal of information about Miniature Railways in the UK.

Although we believe that the information contained in this guide is accurate at the time of going to press, we, and the Railways and Societies itemised, are unable to accept liability for any loss, damage, distress or injury suffered as a result of any inaccuracies. Furthermore, we and the Societies are unable to guarantee operating and opening times which may always be subject to cancellation without notice.

John Robinson

John Robinson

EDITOR

COVER PHOTOGRAPHS

From Standard gauge right down to 7¼ inch gauge, our cover photographs show The Bluebell Railway, the Exbury Gardens Railway and theFrimley Lodge Miniature Railway respectively.

British Library Cataloguing in Publication Data
A catalogue record for this book is available from the British Library

ISBN-13: 978-1-86223-196-2

Copyright © 2010, MARKSMAN PUBLICATIONS. (01472 696226)
72 St. Peter's Avenue, Cleethorpes, N.E. Lincolnshire, DN35 8HU, England

Printed in the UK by The Cromwell Press Group

FOREWORD

Although we are aware that both the Epping Ongar Railway and the Southall Railway Centre were not open to the public when we went to press, we have included them nevertheless as they intend to re-open shortly. However, as with all locations in this book, we recommend that readers check with these railways before planning a visit to avoid disappointment.

The aim of this series of guides is to showcase the great range of UK railways, large and small. In deciding areas covered by this guide we have tried to stick to county boundaries wherever possible but, in a few cases, railways located close to the borders between counties may appear in both this and other guides in the series!

CONTENTS

Railway Locator Maps 2-3
Acknowledgements 4
Foreword and Contents 5-6
Acton Miniature Railway 7
Amberley Museum & Heritage Centre 8
Amnerfield Miniature Railway 9
Audley End Steam Railway 10
Bankside Miniature Railway 11
Barking Park Light Railway 12
Barleylands Miniature Railway 13
Beale Railway 14
Bekonscot Light Railway 15
Bentley Miniature Railway 16
The Bluebell Railway 17
Bolebroke Castle & Lakes Steam Railway 18
Bredgar and Wormshill Light Railway 19
Buckinghamshire Railway Centre 20
Canterbury & District Model Engineering Society 21
Canvey Miniature Railway 22
Chatham Historic Dockyard Railway 23
Chelmsford Society of Model Engineers 24
Chinnor & Princes Risborough Railway 25
Cholsey & Wallingford Railway 26
Colne Valley Railway 27
Crowborough Miniature Railway 28
Cuckoo Hill Railway 29
Cutteslowe Park Miniature Railway 30
Didcot Railway Centre 31
Dockland & East London Model Engineering Society 32
Drusillas Park Railway 33
East Anglian Railway Museum 34
Eastbourne Miniature Steam Railway 35
East Herts Miniature Railway 36
East Kent Railway 37
Eastleigh Lakeside Railway 38
Epping Ongar Railway (Currently closed) 39
Exbury Gardens Railway 40
Fancott Miniature Railway 41
Faversham Miniature Railway 42

Frimley Lodge Miniature Railway 43
Goffs Park Light Railway 44
Golding Spring Miniature Railway 45
Great Cockrow Railway 46
Great Whipsnade Railway 47
Great Woburn Railway 48
Guildford Model Engineering Society Railway 49
Harlington Locomotive Society 50
Hayling Seaside Railway 51
Hollycombe Steam Collection 52
Hotham Park Railway 53
Hythe Ferry Pier Railway 54
Ickenham Miniature Railway 55
Ilford & West Essex Model Railway Club 56
Isle of Wight Steam Railway 57
Kent & East Sussex Railway 58
Knebworth Park Miniature Railway 59
Langford and Beeleigh Railway 60
The Lavender Line 61
Leighton Buzzard Railway 62
Littledown Miniature Railway 63
Mangapps Railway Museum 64
Mid Hants Railway (The Watercress Line) 65
Milton Keynes Light Railway 66
Moors Valley Railway 67
Northolt Model Railway Club 68
Old Kiln Light Railway 69
Paradise Wildlife Park Woodland Railway 70
Pinewood Miniature Railway 71
Reading Society of Model Engineers 72
Romney, Hythe and Dymchurch Railway 73
Roxbourne Park Miniature Railway 74
Royal Victoria Railway 75
Ruislip Lido Railway 76
Saffron Walden & District Society of Model Engineers 77
Southall Railway Centre (Currently closed) 78
South Downs Light Railway 79
Southend Pier Railway 80
Spa Valley Railway 81
Stansted Park Light Railway 82
Summerfields Miniature Railway 83
Surrey Society of Model Engineers 84
Sutton Hall Railway 85
Swanley New Barn Railway 86
Thames Ditton Miniature Railway 87
Tonbridge Model Engineering Society 88
Vanstone Park Miniature Railway 89
Viables Miniature Railway 90
Volks Electric Railway 91
Waterworks Railway 92
Wat Tyler Miniature Railway 93
Wellington Country Park Railway 94
Willen Lake Miniature Railway 95
Woking Miniature Railway 96

ACTON MINIATURE RAILWAY

Address: London Transport Museum Depot, 118 Gunnersbury Lane, London	**Nº of Steam Locos**: Visiting locos only
Telephone Nº: (020) 7379-6344	**Nº of Other Locos**: 1 (plus visiting locos)
Year Formed: 2005	**Nº of Members**: –
Location of Line: Museum Depot	**Approx Nº of Visitors P.A.**: 2,000
Length of Line: 100 yards	**Gauge**: 7¼ inches
	Unofficial web site: www.actonminiaturerailway.co.uk

Photo courtesy of Jonathan James

GENERAL INFORMATION

Nearest Mainline Station: South Acton (¾ mile)
Nearest Tube Station: Acton Town (adjacent)
Car Parking: None
Coach Parking: None
Souvenir Shop(s): None
Food & Drinks: None

SPECIAL INFORMATION

The railway is located in the grounds of the London Transport Museum's Depot in Acton and is operated by Friends of the Museum who helped in the line's construction.

OPERATING INFORMATION

Opening Times: During open weekends only, from 10.30am to 5.00pm. Please check the Museum's web site for further details.
Steam Working: Most opening times
Prices: Adults £1.00
Children £1.00
Concessions £1.00

Detailed Directions by Car:
As there is no parking available at the Depot, it is recommended that visitors take the Underground to Acton Town Station which is adjacent.

AMBERLEY MUSEUM & HERITAGE CENTRE

Address: Amberley Museum & Heritage Centre, Amberley, Arundel BN18 9LT
Telephone Nº: (01798) 831370
Year Formed: 1979
Location of Line: Amberley
Length of Line: ¾ mile

Nº of Steam Locos: 3
Nº of Other Locos: 20+
Nº of Members: 300 volunteers
Annual Membership Fee: £22.00
Approx Nº of Visitors P.A.: 60,000
Gauge: 2 feet
Web site: www.amberleymuseum.co.uk

GENERAL INFORMATION

Nearest Mainline Station: Amberley (adjacent)
Nearest Bus Station: –
Car Parking: Free parking available on site
Coach Parking: Free parking available on site
Souvenir Shop(s): Yes
Food & Drinks: Yes

SPECIAL INFORMATION

Amberley Museum covers 36 acres of former chalk pits and comprises over 30 buildings containing hundreds of different exhibits.

OPERATING INFORMATION

Opening Times: 2010 dates: Tuesday to Sunday from 13th February to 31st October and also on Bank Holidays. Trains run from 10.00am to 5.30pm
Steam Working: Please phone for details.
Prices: Adult £9.30
Child £5.80 (free for Under-5's)
Concessions £8.30
Family £26.50 (2 adults + 3 children)

Detailed Directions by Car:
From All Parts: Amberley Working Museum is situated in West Sussex on the B2139 mid-way between Arundel and Storrington and is adjacent to Amberley Railway Station.

AMNERFIELD MINIATURE RAILWAY

Address: Amners Farm, Burghfield, Berkshire RG30 3UE	**Nº of Steam Locos**: 3
Telephone Nº: (0118) 970-0274	**Nº of Other Locos**: 3
Year Formed: 1995	**Nº of Members**: 7
Location of Line: Amners Farm	**Approx Nº of Visitors P.A.**: 3,000
Length of Line: ¾ mile	**Gauge**: 5 inches and 7¼ inches
	Web site: www.amnersfarm.co.uk

GENERAL INFORMATION

Nearest Mainline Station: Theale (2 miles)
Nearest Bus Station: Reading
Car Parking: Free parking available on site
Coach Parking: None
Souvenir Shop(s): None
Food & Drinks: Available

OPERATING INFORMATION

Opening Times: Easter Sunday then the fourth Sunday in each month from April to October. Trains run from 2.00pm to 5.00pm
Steam Working: Every operating day.
Prices: Adults £1.00
Concessions 50p
Family Ticket £4.00

Detailed Directions by Car:
From All Parts: Exit the M4 at Junction 12 and take the A4 towards Reading. After approximately 2 miles turn right at the traffic lights into Burghfield Road. Continue along this road passing over the motorway then take the first turning on the left into Amners Farm Road. After approximately ½ mile turn right into Amners Farm.

AUDLEY END STEAM RAILWAY

Address: Audley End, Saffron Walden, Essex **Telephone Nº**: (01799) 541354 **Year Formed**: 1964 **Location of Line**: Opposite Audley End House, Saffron Walden	**Length of Line**: 1½ miles **Nº of Steam Locos**: 6 **Nº of Other Locos**: 3 **Nº of Members**: None **Approx Nº of Visitors P.A.**: 42,000 **Gauge**: 10¼ inches **Web site**: www.audley-end-railway.co.uk

GENERAL INFORMATION

Nearest Mainline Station: Audley End (1 mile)
Nearest Bus Station: Saffron Walden (1 mile)
Car Parking: Available on site
Coach Parking: Available on site
Souvenir Shop(s): Yes
Food & Drinks: Snacks available

SPECIAL INFORMATION

Audley End Steam Railway is Lord Braybrooke's private miniature railway situated just next to Audley End House, an English Heritage site. Private parties can be catered for outside of normal running hours.

OPERATING INFORMATION

Opening Times: 2010 dates: Weekends from 27th March to 31st October and also daily during School Holidays. Also Santa Specials in December. Trains run from 2.00pm (11.00am on Bank Holidays).
Steam Working: Weekends and Bank Holidays.
Prices: Adult Return £3.50
   Child Return £2.50
   Santa Specials £5.00
Note: Multi-ride tickets are also available.

Detailed Directions by Car:
Exit the M11 at Junction 10 if southbound or Junction 9 if northbound and follow the signs for Audley End House. The railway is situated just across the road from Audley End House.

BANKSIDE MINIATURE RAILWAY

Address: Brambridge Park Garden Centre, Kiln Lane, Brambridge SO50 6HT	**N° of Steam Locos**: 3
Telephone N°: 07816 773761	**N° of Other Locos**: 1
Year Formed: 1977	**N° of Members**: –
Location of Line: Eastleigh, Hants	**Approx N° of Visitors P.A.**: 5,000
Length of Line: 500 yards	**Gauge**: 8¼ inches and 7¼ inches
	Web site: www.brambridgepark.com

GENERAL INFORMATION

Nearest Mainline Station: Eastleigh (4 miles)
Nearest Bus Station: Eastleigh (4 miles)
Car Parking: Available on site
Coach Parking: Available
Souvenir Shop(s): Yes
Food & Drinks: Available

SPECIAL INFORMATION

The Bankside Miniature Railway runs through the grounds of Brambridge Park Garden Centre which is also the home of the 'Falconhigh' Falconry Display team.

OPERATING INFORMATION

Opening Times: Trains run on weekends and Bank Holidays from Easter until the end of October, from 10.30am to 4.30pm.
Steam Working: All operating days.
Prices: Adults 80p
  Children 80p
  Concessions 80p

Detailed Directions by Car:
From All Parts: Exit the M3 at Junction 12 and take the A335 towards Eastleigh. Turn left at the first roundabout, pass under the railway bridge and the Garden Centre is located on the left after approximately 1 mile.

BARKING PARK LIGHT RAILWAY

Address: Longbridge Road, Barking, IG11 8TA
Telephone Nº: 07768 162258
Year Formed: 2009
Location of Line: Barking Park
Length of Line: 372 yards

Nº of Steam Locos: None
Nº of Other Locos: 3
Nº of Members: –
Approx Nº of Visitors P.A.: Not known
Gauge: 7¼ inches
Web site: www.bplr.co.uk

GENERAL INFORMATION

Nearest Mainline Station: Barking (½ mile)
Nearest Bus Station: Barking (½ mile)
Car Parking: Available on site
Coach Parking: Available
Souvenir Shop(s): None
Food & Drinks: Available

OPERATING INFORMATION

Opening Times: Weekends from Easter until late September and on Mondays in the School Holidays. Trains run from 12.00pm to 6.00pm.
Steam Working: None at present.
Prices: Adult Return 70p
Child Return 70p
Concessionary Return 70p

Detailed Directions by Car:
From All Parts: Barking Park is situated in Longbridge Road, near to the junction of the A124 Northern Relief Road and the A123 Fanshawe Avenue.

BARLEYLANDS MINIATURE RAILWAY

Address: Barleylands, Barleylands Road, Billericay, Essex CM11 2UD **Telephone Nº**: (01268) 290229 **Year Formed**: 1989 **Location of Line**: 3 miles from Billericay **Length of Line**: ¼ mile	**Nº of Steam Locos**: 4 **Nº of Other Locos**: 1 **Nº of Members**: None **Annual Membership Fee**: − **Approx Nº of Visitors P.A.**: 10,000+ **Gauge**: 7¼ inches **Web site**: www.barleylands.co.uk

GENERAL INFORMATION

Nearest Mainline Station: Billericay or Basildon
Nearest Bus Station: Billericay or Basildon
Car Parking: Available on site
Coach Parking: Available on site
Souvenir Shop(s): Yes
Food & Drinks: Yes

SPECIAL INFORMATION

The Railway is located in the Barleylands Craft Village and Farm Centre which has a wide range of attractions for all ages. The railway is commercially operated but volunteers help to run and maintain the steam engines.

OPERATING INFORMATION

Opening Times: Daily throughout the year subject to weather conditions.
Steam Working: The Railway's steam engines may run at a number of special events during 2010. Please contact the railway for further information.
Prices: £1.50 Return (all ages)

Detailed Directions by Car:
From M25: Exit at J29 onto A127 (Southend bound) and follow the brown Tourist Information signs for Farm Museum;   From the A12: Take the B1007 Billericay junction, towards Stock and follow the brown Tourist Information signs for Farm Museum.

BEALE RAILWAY

Address: Beale Park, Lower Basildon, Pangbourne RG8 9NH
Telephone Nº: 0870 777-7160
Year Formed: 1989
Location of Line: Pangbourne, Berks.
Length of Line: Approximately 1 mile

Nº of Steam Locos: 1
Nº of Other Locos: 1
Approx Nº of Visitors P.A.: –
Gauge: 10¼ inches
Web site: www.bealepark.co.uk

GENERAL INFORMATION

Nearest Mainline Station: Pangbourne (1 mile)
Nearest Bus Station: Reading (12 miles)
Car Parking: Available on site
Coach Parking: Available on site
Souvenir Shop(s): Yes
Food & Drinks: Available

SPECIAL INFORMATION

The railway is situated within Child-Beale Trust, Beale Park alongside the River Thames. The Park has numerous other attractions including collections of small exotic animals, farm animals & birds, landscaped gardens & woodlands and play areas.

OPERATING INFORMATION

Opening Times: Beale Park is open daily from the 1st March to 31st October. Open from 10.00am to 5.00pm in March and October and until 6.00pm at other times. The first train departs at 10.30am daily and the last train departs 15 minutes before Beale Park closes.

Steam Working: Trains may be steam or diesel-hauled depending on operational needs.
Prices: One free ride is included in the park admission fee. All rides thereafter are £1.00 each.
Park Admission: Adults £6.00 or £8.50
Children £4.00 or £6.00
Senior Citizens £5.00 or £7.00
Note: The lower prices shown above are valid only for March and October. The higher prices shown are charged between April and September.

Detailed Directions by Car:
Beale Park is situated just off the A329 Reading to Goring Road at Pangbourne.

BEKONSCOT LIGHT RAILWAY

Address: Bekonscot Model Village & Railway, Warwick Road, Beaconsfield, Bucks   HP9 2PL
Telephone Nº: (01494) 672919
Year Formed: 2001
Location of Line: Beaconsfield, Bucks.
Length of Line: 400 yards

Nº of Steam Locos: None at present
Nº of Other Locos: 3
Nº of Members: –
Approx Nº of Visitors P.A.: 180,000
Gauge: 7¼ inches
Web site: www.bekonscot.com

GENERAL INFORMATION

Nearest Mainline Station:
Beaconsfield (5 minutes walk)
Nearest Bus Station: High Wycombe
Car Parking: Limited spaces adjacent to the site
Coach Parking: Limited spaces adjacent to the site
Souvenir Shop(s): Yes
Food & Drinks: Available

SPECIAL INFORMATION

The Railway is situated in Bekonscot Model Village, a 1½ acre miniature landscape of fields, farms, castles, churches, woods and lakes which also contains a model railway.

OPERATING INFORMATION

Opening Times: Daily from mid-February to 1st November. Open 10.00am to 5.00pm.
Steam Working: None at present
Prices: Adult £8.50
          Child £5.00 (Ages 2–15 years)
          Family Ticket £25.00
          Senior Citizen/Concessions £6.00
Note: Prices shown above are for entrance into Bekonscot Model Village which is required to visit the railway. Rides are an additional 90p per person.

Detailed Directions by Car:
From All Parts: Exit the M40 at Junction 2 taking the A355 then follow the signs for the "Model Village".

BENTLEY MINIATURE RAILWAY

Address: Bentley Wildfowl & Motor Museum, Halland   BN8 5AF
Telephone Nº: (01825) 762783
Year Formed: 1985
Location of Line: 5 miles North of Lewes
Length of Line: ½ mile

Nº of Steam Locos: Members locos only
Nº of Other Locos: Members locos only
Approx Nº of Visitors P.A.: 50,000 (to the Museum)
Gauge: 5 inches and 7¼ inches
Web site: www.bentleyrailway.co.uk

GENERAL INFORMATION

Nearest Mainline Station: Uckfield (4 miles)
Nearest Bus Station: Uckfield (4 miles)
Car Parking: Free parking available on site
Coach Parking: Free parking available on site
Souvenir Shop(s): Yes
Food & Drinks: Available

SPECIAL INFORMATION

The railway is owned and operated by members of the Uckfield Model Railway Club and is located in the grounds of the Bentley Wildfowl & Motor Museum (www.bentley.org.uk) which houses a wide range of other attractions.

OPERATING INFORMATION

Opening Times: Sundays throughout the year. Weekends from Easter to the end of October and daily during most East Sussex School Holidays throughout the year. Trains run from 11.00am to 4.00pm (5.00pm from Easter to end of October).
Steam Working: Most Sundays.
Prices: Adults £7.50 (Museum Entry only)
Children £5.50 (Museum Entry only)
Concessions £6.50 (Museum Entry only)
Family £25.00 (Museum Entry only)
Note: Train rides are an additional 80p per person.

Detailed Directions by Car:
From All Parts: Bentley Wildfowl & Motor Museum is located just outside of the village of Shortgate by the B2192 road between Halland (which located by at the junction of the B2192 and A22) and Lewes (A26/A27). The Museum is well-signposted locally from the A22 (Uckfield to Eastbourne), A26 (Uckfield to Lewes) and B2192.

THE BLUEBELL RAILWAY

Address: The Bluebell Railway, Sheffield Park Station, Nr. Uckfield, East Sussex, TN22 3QL
Telephone Nº: (01825) 720800
Information Line: (01825) 720825
Year Formed: 1959
Location of Line: Nr. Uckfield, E. Sussex
Length of Line: 9 miles

Nº of Steam Locos: Over 30 with up to 3 in operation on any given day
Nº of Other Locos: –
Nº of Members: 10,000
Annual Membership Fee: £20.00 Adult
Approx Nº of Visitors P.A.: 175,000
Gauge: Standard
Web site: www.bluebell-railway.co.uk

Photo courtesy of David Staines

GENERAL INFORMATION

Nearest Mainline Station: East Grinstead (2 miles) with a bus connection
Nearest Bus Station: East Grinstead
Car Parking: Parking at Sheffield Park and Horsted Keynes Stations.
Coach Parking: Sheffield Park is best
Souvenir Shop(s): Yes
Food & Drinks: Yes – buffets and licensed bars & restaurant

SPECIAL INFORMATION

The Railway runs 'Golden Arrow' dining trains on Saturday evenings and Sunday lunchtimes. There is also a museum and model railway at Sheffield Park Station.

OPERATING INFORMATION

Opening Times: 2010 dates: Open every weekend throughout the year and also daily from 2nd April to 7th November inclusive. Also open during School holidays and for Santa Specials during December. Open from approximately 10.30am to 5.30pm
Steam Working: As above
Prices: Adult Return £12.00
Child Return £6.00
Family Return £33.00 (2 adult + 3 child)

Detailed Directions by Car:
Sheffield Park Station is situated on the A275 Wych Cross to Lewes road. Horsted Keynes Station is signposted from the B2028 Lingfield to Haywards Heath road.

BOLEBROKE CASTLE & LAKES STEAM RAILWAY

Address: Bolebroke Castle, Edenbridge Road, Hartfield, East Sussex TN7 4JJ
Telephone Nº: (01892) 770061
Year Formed: 1984
Location of Line: Bolebroke Castle
Length of Line: ½ mile

Nº of Steam Locos: 7
Nº of Other Locos: 8
Nº of Members: Approximately 36
Annual Membership Fee: £20.00
Approx Nº of Visitors P.A.: –
Gauge: 7¼ inches

GENERAL INFORMATION

Nearest Mainline Station: Tunbridge Wells
Nearest Bus Station: Hartfield
Car Parking: Available on site
Coach Parking: Available on site
Souvenir Shop(s): Yes
Food & Drinks: Yes

SPECIAL INFORMATION

The Railway runs around a lake situated in the grounds of a historic 15th Century Castle. Entrance to the castle is restricted so please phone for details of opening times.

OPERATING INFORMATION

Opening Times: Weekends from April to October and daily during the School holidays.
Steam Working: Some Sundays – phone for details
Prices: Admission to the grounds of the castle is free of charge. The cost of rides are as follows:
  Adult £2.50
  Child £1.50

Detailed Directions by Car:
From All Parts: Take the A264 from Tunbridge Wells towards East Grinstead and turn off for Hartfield on either the B2110 (via Groombridge) or the B2026. Follow signs for Bolebroke Castle for the railway.

BREDGAR & WORMSHILL LIGHT RAILWAY

Address: The Warren, Bredgar,
near Sittingbourne, Kent   ME9 8AT
Telephone Nº: (01622) 884254
Year Formed: 1972
Location of Line: 1 mile south of Bredgar
Gauge: 2 feet
Length of Line: ¾ mile

Nº of Steam Locos: 10
Nº of Other Locos: 2
Nº of Members: –
Annual Membership Fee: –
Approx Nº of Visitors P.A.: 7,000
Web site: www.bwlr.co.uk

GENERAL INFORMATION

Nearest Mainline Station:
Hollingbourne (3 miles) or Sittingbourne (5 miles)
Nearest Bus Station: Sittingbourne
Car Parking: 500 spaces available – free parking
Coach Parking: Free parking available by
appointment
Souvenir Shop(s): Yes
Food & Drinks: Yes

SPECIAL INFORMATION

A small but beautiful railway in rural Kent. The
railway also has other attractions including a Model
Railway, Traction Engines, a working Beam Engine,
Vintage cars, a Locomotive Shed, a picnic site and
woodland walks.

OPERATING INFORMATION

Opening Times: Open on Easter Sunday then the
first Sunday of the month from May to October.
Open from 10.30am to 5.00pm
Steam Working: 11.00am to 4.30pm
Prices: Adult £7.50   Child £3.00

Detailed Directions by Car:
Take the M20 and exit at Junction 8 (Leeds Castle exit). Travel 4½ miles due north through Hollingbourne. The
Railway is situated a little over 1 mile south of Bredgar village.

BUCKINGHAMSHIRE RAILWAY CENTRE

Address: Quainton Road Station, Quainton, Aylesbury, Bucks. HP22 4BY **Telephone Nº:** (01296) 655720 **Year Formed:** 1969 **Location of Line:** At Quainton on the old Metropolitan/Great Central Line **Length of Line:** 2 × ½ mile demo tracks	**Nº of Steam Locos:** 30 **Nº of Other Locos:** 6 **Nº of Members:** 1,000 **Annual Membership Fee:** £20.00 **Approx Nº of Visitors P.A.:** 40,000 **Gauge:** Standard (also a Miniature line) **Recorded Info. Line:** (01296) 655450

GENERAL INFORMATION

Nearest Mainline Station: Aylesbury (6 miles)
Nearest Bus Station: Aylesbury
Car Parking: Free parking for 500 cars available
Coach Parking: Free parking for 10 coaches
Souvenir Shop(s): Yes
Food & Drinks: Yes

SPECIAL INFORMATION

In addition to a large collection of locomotives and carriages, the Centre has an extensive ½ mile outdoor miniature railway system operated by the Vale of Aylesbury Model Engineering Society.

Web site: www.bucksrailcentre.org

OPERATING INFORMATION

Opening Times: Daily for restricted viewing from Easter to October and for less restricted static viewing on Saturdays. Open 10.30am to 4.30pm.
Steam Working: Sundays and Bank Holidays from April to October and also on Wednesdays during the School holidays.
Prices: Adult £5.50, £8.00 and £9.00
        Child £3.00, £5.00 and £6.00
        (Under 5's travel free of charge)
        Senior Citizen £5.00, £7.00 and £8.00
        Family £14.00, £21.00 and £24.00
        (2 adults + up to 4 children)
Note: Prices shown above are for static viewing, Steam Days and Special Event days respectively.

Detailed Directions by Car:
The Buckinghamshire Railway Centre is signposted off the A41 Aylesbury to Bicester Road at Waddesdon and off the A413 Buckingham to Aylesbury road at Whitchurch. Junctions 7, 8 and 9 of the M40 are all close by.

CANTERBURY & DISTRICT M.E.S.

Address: Brett Quarry, Fordwich,
Near Canterbury, Kent
Phone Nº: (01227) 830081 (Secretary)
Year Formed: 1972
Location of Line: Brett Quarry, Fordwich
Length of Line: 750 feet

Nº of Steam Locos: (As provided by the
Nº of Other Locos: MES members)
Nº of Members: Approximately 60
Gauge: 3½ inches and 5 inches
Web site: www.cdmes.org.uk

GENERAL INFORMATION

Nearest Mainline Station: Sturry (½ mile)
Nearest Bus Station: Canterbury (3 miles)
Car Parking: None on site
Coach Parking: None
Food & Drinks: None

SPECIAL INFORMATION

The Canterbury & District Model Engineering
Society runs a track on land kindly loaned by Bretts
of Fordwich which is open to the public on some
Sunday afternoons throughout the year, weather
permitting.

OPERATING INFORMATION

Opening Times: 2010 dates: 11th April, 9th May,
13th June, 11th July, 8th August, 12th September and
10th October. Trains run from 2.00pm to 5.00pm,
weather permitting.
Steam Working: Most operating days depending on
which locos have been provided by the MES
members.
Prices: Free rides although donations are accepted
for the upkeep of the track.

Detailed Directions by Car:
From the A28 at Sturry turn into Fordwich Road then left into Marlowe Meadows (look for the Brett sign). Drive
towards the large green gates then walk through following the access road. Please note that the railway is on
private land and access to the public is limited so please do not drive down this road as there is no parking on-site.

CANVEY MINIATURE RAILWAY

Address: Waterside Farm Sports Centre, Somnes Avenue, Canvey Island, Essex, SS8 9RA
Telephone Nº: (01268) 681679
Year Formed: 1977
Location of Line: Canvey Island
Length of Line: Two lines, one of 1,440 feet and one of 4,400 feet (7¼ inch line)

Nº of Steam Locos: Variable
Nº of Other Locos: Variable
Nº of Members: Approximately 100
Approx Nº of Visitors P.A.: 6,000
Gauge: 3½ inches, 5 inches & 7¼ inches
Web site: www.cramec.org

GENERAL INFORMATION

Nearest Mainline Station: Benfleet (1 mile)
Nearest Bus Station: Bus stop just outside
Car Parking: Available on site
Coach Parking: Available on site
Food & Drinks: None

SPECIAL INFORMATION

The railway is operated by members of the Canvey Railway and Model Engineering Club.

OPERATING INFORMATION

Opening Times: Every Sunday from the first Sunday in April until the second Sunday in October. Trains run from 10.30am to 4.00pm.
Steam Working: When available on operating days.
Prices: £1.00 per ride.
Also £5.00 for 6 rides or £9.00 for 12 rides.

Detailed Directions by Car:
All road routes to Canvey Island meet at the Waterside Farm roundabout. The railway lines are located in the grounds of the Sports Complex/Leisure Centre. Turn right at the traffic lights into the centre and the car park is on the left with the railway on the right.

CHATHAM HISTORIC DOCKYARD RAILWAY

Address: Dock Road, Chatham
Telephone Nº: (01634) 823800
Year Formed: 2001
Location of Line: Chatham, Kent
Length of Line: ¾ mile

Nº of Steam Locos: 5
Nº of Other Locos: 3
Nº of Members: –
Approx Nº of Visitors P.A.: Not known
Gauge: Standard
Web site: www.thedockyardrailway.co.uk

GENERAL INFORMATION

Nearest Mainline Station: Chatham (1½ miles)
Nearest Bus Station: Gillingham (1½ miles)
Car Parking: Available on site
Coach Parking: Available
Souvenir Shop(s): Yes
Food & Drinks: Available

SPECIAL INFORMATION

The Dockyard Railway is operated by North Kent
Industrial Locomotive Society and runs
demonstrations of freight steaming at Chatham's
Historic Dockyard (www.chdt.org.uk).

OPERATING INFORMATION

Opening Times: Open one weekend per month.
Please telephone or check the web site for details of
special event dates.
Steam Working: Most operating days. Please note
that the Railway does not offer train rides, merely
demonstrations of engines in operation.
Prices: Adults £15.00
Children (Aged 5-15 years old) £10.50
Concessions £12.50
Family Tickets £42.50
Note: Prices shown are for admission to the
Dockyard and tickets are valid for 12 months.
However, entrance to some special events is an
additional charge.

Detailed Directions by Car:
From All Parts: Exit the M2 at Junction 3 and follow the A229 to Chatham. Follow the Brown tourist signs which
clearly mark the correct route to the Dockyard.

CHELMSFORD SOCIETY MODEL ENGINEERS

Address: Meteor Way (off Waterhouse Lane), Chelmsford, Essex CM1 2RL
Telephone Nº: None
Year Formed: 1935
Location of Line: Chelmsford
Length of Line: Two tracks, each approximately 1,000 feet long

Nº of Steam Locos: 40+ (owned by
Nº of Other Locos: 10+ members)
Nº of Members: Approximately 75
Approx Nº of Visitors P.A.: 1,500
Gauge: 3½ inches, 5 inches & 7¼ inches
Web site:
www.chelmsford-miniature-railway.org.uk

GENERAL INFORMATION

Nearest Mainline Station: Chelmsford (½ mile)
Nearest Bus Station: Chelmsford (½ mile)
Car Parking: Available adjacent to the railway (currently free of charge at weekends)
Food & Drinks: Light refreshments available

SPECIAL INFORMATION

The Chelmsford Society of Model Engineers promotes the safe construction and operation of passenger-carrying steam, electric and diesel hauled trains, traction engines and other scale models.

OPERATING INFORMATION

Opening Times: 2010 dates: Every Sunday from 25th April to 26th September inclusive. Also Children in Need Day on 14th November (11.30am to 3.30pm) and Santa Specials on 5th December. Trains usually run from 2.00pm to 4.30pm. Please check the Society's web site for further details.
Steam Working: Most operating days.
Prices: 50p per person per ride. 12 rides are available for the price of £5.00

Detailed Directions by Car:
From London: Follow the A12 then take the A1016 towards Chelmsford town centre. Continue past the A414 junctions into Westway then into Waterhouse Lane. Meteor Way is on the right after the fourth set of traffic lights, just before the river. Park and then proceed past the five bar gate to the club entrance on the right; From Southend: Follow the A130 to the A12 junction then cross onto the A1114. After 1¼ miles join the A414 towards Chelmsford. Follow the A414 around Chelmsford to the junction with the A1016 at Widford. Take the 2nd exit into Westway then as from London; From Colchester: Follow the A12 and exit at the A414 junction towards Chelmsford. Follow the A414 to the A1016, then as from Southend.

CHINNOR & PRINCES RISBOROUGH RAILWAY

Address: Station Road, Chinnor, Oxon, OX39 4ER **Telephone Nº**: (01844) 353535 (timetable) **Year Formed**: 1989 **Location**: The Icknield Line, Chinnor **Length of Line**: 3½ miles **Gauge**: Standard	**Nº of Steam Locos**: 1 **Nº of Other Locos**: 6 **Nº of Members**: 1,000 **Annual Membership Fee**: Adult £13.00; Family £20.00; Child £5.00; OAP £8.00 **Approx Nº of Visitors P.A.**: 15,000 **Web Site**: www.chinnorrailway.co.uk

Photo courtesy of Peter Harris

GENERAL INFORMATION

Nearest Mainline Station: Princes Risborough (4 miles)
Nearest Bus Station: High Wycombe (10 miles)
Car Parking: Free parking at site
Coach Parking: Prior arrangement preferred but not necessary
Souvenir Shop(s): Yes
Food & Drinks: Soft drinks and light snacks in Station Buffet. Buffet usually available on trains.

SPECIAL INFORMATION

The Chinnor & Princes Risborough Railway operates the remaining 3½ mile section of the former GWR Watlington Branch from Chinnor to Thame Junction.

OPERATING INFORMATION

Opening Times: 2010 dates: Sundays and Bank Holiday Mondays from 14th March to 31st October and also Santa Specials on weekends in December. Also open on selected Saturdays between April and August. Please check the railway's website for details.
Steam Working: Operates from 10.15am to 4.15pm on Sundays.
Prices: Adult Return £9.00
Child Return £4.50
Family Return £22.50 (2 adult + 2 child)
Senior Citizen Return £8.00

Detailed Directions by Car:
From All Parts: The railway at Chinnor is situated in Station Road just off the B4009. Junction 6 of the M40 is 4 miles away and Princes Risborough 4 miles further along the B4009. Once in Chinnor follow the brown Tourist signs to the railway.

CHOLSEY & WALLINGFORD RAILWAY

Address: Wallingford Station,
5 Hithercroft Road, Wallingford, Oxon,
OX10 9GQ
Telephone No: (01491) 835067 (24hr info)
Year Formed: 1981
Location of Line: Wallingford, Oxon.
Length of Line: 2½ miles

No of Steam Locos: Visiting locos only
No of Other Locos: 4
No of Members: 250
Annual Membership Fee: £12.50
Approx No of Visitors P.A.: 9,700
Gauge: Standard
Web: www.cholsey-wallingford-railway.com

GENERAL INFORMATION

Nearest Mainline Station: Joint station at Cholsey
Nearest Bus Station: Wallingford (¼ mile)
Car Parking: Off road parking available
Coach Parking: Off road parking available
Souvenir Shop(s): Yes
Food & Drinks: Yes

SPECIAL INFORMATION

The Wallingford branch (now known as "The Bunk
Line") was originally intended as a through line to
Princes Risborough, via Watlington, but became the
first standard gauge branch of Brunel's broad-gauge
London to Bristol line.

OPERATING INFORMATION

Opening Times: Selected weekends from Easter
until Christmas with trains running from 11.00am
to 4.30pm – please phone the railway or check the
web site for further details.
Steam Working: The railway will have a visiting
steam locomotive which will commence operation
from June 2010. Please contact the railway for
further information.
Prices: Adult Return £6.00
Child Return £3.00
Concessionary Return £5.00
Family Return £16.00 (2 adult + 2 child)
Prices: Prices may be subject to change for Engine
visits and other special events.

Detailed Directions by Car:
From All Parts: Exit from the A34 at the Milton Interchange (between E. Ilsley and Abingdon). Follow signs to
Didcot and Wallingford (A4130). Take Wallingford bypass, then turn left at the first roundabout (signposted
Hithercroft Road). The Station is then ½ mile on the right.

COLNE VALLEY RAILWAY

Address: Castle Hedingham Station, Yeldham Road, Castle Hedingham, Essex, CO9 3DZ
Telephone Nº: (01787) 461174
Year Formed: 1974
Location of Line: On A1017, 7 miles north-west of Braintree
Length of Line: Approximately 1 mile

Nº of Steam Locos: 4
Nº of Other Locos: 11
Nº of Members: 280
Annual Membership Fee: £11.00
Approx Nº of Visitors P.A.: 45,000
Gauge: Standard
Web Site: www.colnevalleyrailway.co.uk

GENERAL INFORMATION

Nearest Mainline Station: Braintree (7 miles)
Nearest Bus Station: Hedingham bus from Braintree stops at the Railway (except on Sundays)
Car Parking: Parking at the site
Coach Parking: Free parking at site
Souvenir Shop(s): Yes
Food & Drinks: Yes – on operational days. Also Pullman Sunday Lunches – bookings necessary.

SPECIAL INFORMATION

The railway is being re-built on a section of the old Colne Valley & Halstead Railway, with all buildings, bridges, signal boxes, etc. re-located on site. The Railway also has a Farm Park on site which is open from early May until early October.

OPERATING INFORMATION

Opening Times: 2010 dates: Trains run every Sunday and Bank Holiday weekend from 28th March to 3rd October. Open daily in August except for Mondays and Fridays. Pre-booked parties any time by arrangement and various other special events. Please check the web site for further details.
Steam Working: Sundays 10.30pm to 4.00pm, Bank Holidays from 10.30am to 4.00pm and 10.30am to 4.30pm on midweek operating days.
Prices: Adult – Steam days £8.00; Diesel £6.00
Child – Steam £5.00; Diesel £4.00
Family (2 adults + 4 children) –
Steam £28.00; Diesel £22.00
Senior Citizen – Steam £7.00; Diesel £5.00

Detailed Directions by Car:
The Railway is situated on the A1017 between Halstead and Haverhill, 7 miles north-west of Braintree.

CROWBOROUGH MINIATURE RAILWAY

Address: Goldsmiths Leisure Centre, Eridge Road, Crowborough   TN6 2TN
Telephone Nº: (01892) 852741
Year Formed: 1990
Location of Line: Crowborough
Length of Line: ¼ mile circuit

Nº of Steam Locos: Members locos only
Nº of Other Locos: 1
Nº of Members: 30
Approx Nº of Visitors P.A.: 900
Gauge: 3½ inches and 5 inches
Web site: www.crowborough-mini-railway.vze.com

GENERAL INFORMATION
Nearest Mainline Station: Crowborough (1½ miles)
Nearest Bus Station: Tunbridge Wells (7 miles)
Car Parking: Available on site
Coach Parking: Available on site
Food & Drinks: Available at the Leisure Centre

SPECIAL INFORMATION
The Crowborough Locomotive Society was formed to build, maintain, and run a miniature railway at the Goldsmiths Leisure Centre in Crowborough. The society runs live steam working locomotives to give both young and old alike a railway journey in miniature!

OPERATING INFORMATION
Opening Times: Saturday afternoons and selected Sundays from Easter until early November. Trains run from 2.30pm to 4.45pm.
Steam Working: Most operational days, depending on which members' locos are running.
Prices: £1.00 per person for two circuits of the track.

Detailed Directions by Car:
Goldsmiths Leisure Centre is situated in the north of Crowborough just off the A26 (Eridge Road) which is the main Tunbridge Wells to Uckfield through road.

CUCKOO HILL RAILWAY

Address: Avon Valley Nurseries, South Gorley SP6 2PP	**N⁰ of Steam Locos:** 1
Telephone N⁰: (01425) 650408	**N⁰ of Other Locos:** None
Year Formed: 1991	**N⁰ of Members:** –
Location: Near Ringwood, Hampshire	**Approx N⁰ of Visitors P.A.:** 7,000
Length of Line: 900 yards	**Gauge:** 7¼ inches
	Web site: None

GENERAL INFORMATION

Nearest Mainline Station: Salisbury (12 miles)
Nearest Bus Station: Salisbury (12 miles)
Car Parking: Available on site
Coach Parking: Available in the Village
Souvenir Shop(s): None
Food & Drinks: Available

SPECIAL INFORMATION

Cuckoo Hill Railway is one of the earliest railways to operate at a garden centre in the UK.

OPERATING INFORMATION

Opening Times: Weekends and Bank Holiday Mondays from March to the end of October. Also open on Thursdays and Fridays during the School Holidays. Trains run from 11.30am to 5.00pm.
Steam Working: Every operating day.
Prices: £1.25 per ride

Detailed Directions by Car:
From All Parts: South Gorley is situated on the A338 between Ringwood and Fordingbridge and the Nurseries are just to the east of the road.

CUTTESLOWE PARK MINIATURE RAILWAY

Address: Cutteslowe Park, Harbord Road, Oxford   OX2 8ES
Phone Nº: (01367) 700550 (Secretary)
Year Formed: 1955
Location: Cutteslowe Park, Oxford
Length of Line: Two lines – 390 yard raised line and 250 yard ground level line

Nº of Steam Locos: 40
Nº of Other Locos: 10
Nº of Members: Approximately 110
Approx Nº of Visitors P.A.: 10,000
Gauge: 3½ inches, 5 inches & 7¼ inches
Web site: www.cosme.org.uk

GENERAL INFORMATION

Nearest Mainline Station: Oxford (3¼ miles)
Nearest Bus Station: Oxford (3 miles)
Car Parking: Available on site
Coach Parking: Available by prior arrangement
Food & Drinks: Refreshments are available in Cutteslowe Park

SPECIAL INFORMATION

The Cutteslowe Park Miniature Railway is operated by the City of Oxford Society of Model Engineers.

OPERATING INFORMATION

Opening Times: The railway opens on the 1st, 3rd and 5th Sundays of each month as well as Bank Holidays from Easter to the end of October. Trains run from 1.30pm to 5.00pm. Trains also run on Wednesdays in the School Summer Holidays in July and August – 1.00pm to 4.30pm.
Steam Working: Up to 5 steam locomotives run on every operating day.
Prices: Adults £1.00   Children £1.00
          10 rides are available for £8.00

Detailed Directions by Car:
From outside of Oxford join the ringroad and head to the North of the city. At the roundabout at the junction of the A40 ringroad and the A4165 Banbury Road, head North signposted for Kidlington. Take the third turn on the right into Harbord Road which leads directly into the Park. Follow the signs from the car park for the Railway.

DIDCOT RAILWAY CENTRE

Address: Didcot Railway Centre, Didcot, Oxfordshire OX11 7NJ **Telephone Nº:** (01235) 817200 **Year Formed:** 1961 **Location of Line:** Didcot **Length of Line:** ¾ mile **Gauge:** Standard and 7 foot ¼ inch	**Nº of Steam Locos:** 23 **Nº of Other Locos:** 2 **Nº of Members:** 4,400 **Annual Membership Fee:** Full £26.00; Over 60/Under 18 £18.00; Family £33.00 **Approx Nº of Visitors P.A.:** 70,000 **Web Site:** www.didcotrailwaycentre.org.uk

GENERAL INFO

Nearest Mainline Station: Didcot Parkway (adjacent)

Nearest Bus Station: Buses to Didcot call at the Railway station

Car Parking: BR car park adjacent

Coach Parking: Further details on application

Souvenir Shop(s): Yes

Food & Drinks: Yes

SPECIAL INFO

The Centre is based on a Great Western Railway engine shed and is devoted to the re-creation of part of the GWR including Brunel's broad gauge railway and a newly built replica of the Fire Fly locomotive of 1840.

OPERATING INFO

Opening Times: 2010 dates: Weekends all year round, open daily during most school holidays and then from 1st June to 12th September. Weekends and Steam days open 10.30am to 5.00pm. Other days and during Winter open 10.30am to 4.00pm.

Steam Working: Bank Holidays and most weekends until 30th August. Wednesdays from 21st July to 25th August. Phone or check the web site for details of Autumn steam days.

Prices: Adult £5.00–£10.00
Child £4.00–£10.00
Discounted family tickets are often available (2 adults + 2 children). Prices vary depending on the events.

Detailed Directions by Car:
From East & West: Take the M4 to Junction 13 then the A34 and A4130 (follow brown Tourist signs to Didcot Railway Centre); From North: The Centre is signed from the A34 to A4130.

DOCKLAND & EAST LONDON M.E.S.

Address: Belhus Woods Country Park, Romford Road, Aveley, Essex **Phone Nº:** (01708) 222658 (Secretary) **Year Formed:** 1985 **Location:** Belhus Woods Country park **Length of Line:** 500 feet	**Nº of Steam Locos:** 3 **Nº of Other Locos:** 3 **Nº of Members:** 32 **Approx Nº of Visitors P.A.:** 400 **Gauge:** 5 inches and 7¼ inches

GENERAL INFORMATION

Nearest Mainline Station: Upminster (4 miles)
Nearest Bus Station: Grays (5 miles). Arriva bus service 373 will stop at Belhus Woods and collect passengers there on request although there is no stop.
Car Parking: Pay & Display parking available on site
Coach Parking: Available by prior arrangement
Souvenir Shop(s): Yes – Country Park shop
Food & Drinks: Light refreshments available

SPECIAL INFORMATION

The Railway is located in Belhus Woods which is a beautiful Country Park which has barbecue areas adjacent to the track and woodland walks through areas full of waterfowl.

OPERATING INFORMATION

Opening Times: During the first Sunday of every month from April to October inclusive. Also on the first Saturday in June, July & August. Trains run from 1.00pm to 4.30pm.
Steam Working: Both Steam-hauled and Electric services run on every operating day.
Prices: 50p per person per ride.

Detailed Directions by Car:
Exit the M25 at Junction 29 and follow the A127 towards Romford. After 1 mile turn off at the Hall Lane exit by the flyover and head South towards Upminster. Continue down Hall Lane following through into Station Road then Corbets Tey Road. Upon reaching the T-junction turn right into Harwood Hall Lane then left at the mini-roundabout into Aveley Road. Belhus Woods Country Park is on the left after about 1¼ miles.

DRUSILLAS PARK RAILWAY

Address: Alfriston Road, Alfriston,
BN26 5QS
Telephone Nº: (01323) 874100
Year Formed: –
Location of Line: Drusillas Park
Length of Line: 370 yards

Nº of Steam Locos: None
Nº of Other Locos: 1
Nº of Members: –
Approx Nº of Visitors P.A.: 375,000
(visitors to the Park)
Gauge: 2 feet
Web site: www.drusillas.co.uk

GENERAL INFORMATION

Nearest Mainline Station: Berwick (1 mile)
Nearest Bus Station: Eastbourne (7 miles)
Car Parking: Available on site
Coach Parking: Available
Souvenir Shop(s): Yes
Food & Drinks: Available

SPECIAL INFORMATION

Drusillas Park offers daily Thomas and Friends train
rides in addition to a wide range of other attractions
for children including a Zoo and an adventure
playground.

OPERATING INFORMATION

Opening Times: Daily except for Christmas Eve,
Christmas Day and Boxing Day. Open from 10.00am
to 5.00pm (until 6.00pm in the Summer).
Steam Working: None at present.
Prices: Park entry prices depend on season:
Adults £11.30 to £14.30
Children £10.80 to £13.80
Concessions £10.80 to £13.80
Family Tickets £21.60 to £69.00
(A variety of family tickets are available)

Detailed Directions by Car:
From All Parts: Drusillas is situated just off the A27 Eastbourne to Lewes road, near Alfriston. The Park is clearly
signposted from the A27.

EAST ANGLIAN RAILWAY MUSEUM

Address: Chappel & Wakes Colne Station, Colchester, Essex CO6 2DS
Telephone Nº: (01206) 242524
Year Formed: 1969
Location of Line: 6 miles west of Colchester on Marks Tey to Sudbury branch
Length of Line: A third of a mile

Nº of Steam Locos: 5 **Other Locos:** 4
Nº of Members: 750
Annual Membership Fee: Adult £20.00; Senior Citizen £15.00
Approx Nº of Visitors P.A.: 40,000
Gauge: Standard
Web site: www.earm.co.uk

GENERAL INFORMATION

Nearest Mainline Station: Chappel & Wakes Colne (adajcent)
Nearest Bus Stop: Chappel (400 yards)
Car Parking: Free parking at site
Coach Parking: Free parking at site
Souvenir Shop(s): Yes
Food & Drinks: Yes – drinks are available every day and snacks are also available on operating days.

SPECIAL INFORMATION

The museum has the most comprehensive collection of railway architecture & engineering in the region. The railway also has a miniature railway that usually operates on steam days.

OPERATING INFORMATION

Opening Times: Open daily 10.00am to 4.30pm. Steam days open from 11.00am to 4.30pm. Closed on Christmas Day and Boxing Day.
Steam Working: Steam days are held every month from April to August and also in October and December. Bank Holidays are also Steam days. Check the web site for further details.
Prices: Adult £4.00 non-Steam; £8.00 Steam
Child £2.00 non-Steam; £4.00 Steam
O.A.P. £3.50 non-Steam; £7.00 Steam
Family £10.00 non-Steam; £20.00 Steam
Children under the age of 4 are admitted free of charge. A 10% discount is available for bookings for more than 10 people. A 10% discount is also available for visitors who visit using Mainline trains!

Detailed Directions by Car:
From North & South: Turn off the A12 south west of Colchester onto the A1124 (formerly the A604). The Museum is situated just off the A1124; From West: Turn off the A120 just before Marks Tey (signposted).

EASTBOURNE MINIATURE STEAM RAILWAY

Address: Lottbridge Drove, Eastbourne, East Sussex BN23 6QJ	**Nº of Steam Locos:** 6
Telephone Nº: (01323) 520229	**Nº of Other Locos:** 3
Year Formed: 1992	**Nº of Members:** –
Location of Line: Eastbourne	**Approx Nº of Visitors P.A.:** –
Length of Line: 1 mile	**Gauge:** 7¼ inches
	Web site: www.emsr.co.uk

GENERAL INFORMATION

Nearest Mainline Station: Eastbourne (2 miles)
Nearest Bus Station: Eastbourne (2 miles)
Car Parking: Free parking on site
Coach Parking: Free parking on site
Souvenir Shop(s): Yes
Food & Drinks: Yes

SPECIAL INFORMATION

The Railway site also has many other attractions including model railways, an adventure playground, nature walk, maze, picnic area and a Cafe.

OPERATING INFORMATION

Opening Times: 2010 dates: Open 10.00am to 5.00pm daily from 27th March until 3rd October. Also special events on Easter Sunday.
Steam Working: Weekends, Bank Holidays and during School Holidays. Diesel at other times.
Prices: Adult £4.45
      Child £3.95 (2 years and under free)
      Family Tickets £16.00
            (2 adults + 2 children)

Detailed Directions by Car:
From All Parts: Take the A22 new road to Eastbourne then follow the Brown tourist signs for the 'Mini Railway'.

EAST HERTS MINIATURE RAILWAY

Address: Van Hage Garden Centre, Great Amwell, near Ware SG12 9RP **Telephone Nº**: (020) 8292-2997 **Year Formed**: 1978 **Location**: Van Hage Garden Centre **Length of Line**: 500 metres	**Nº of Steam Locos**: 3 **Nº of Other Locos**: 2 **Nº of Members**: Approximately 40 **Annual Membership Fee**: £16.00 **Approx Nº of Visitors P.A.**: 40,000 **Gauge**: 7¼ inches **Web site**: www.ehmr.org.uk

GENERAL INFORMATION

Nearest Mainline Station: Ware (1½ miles)
Nearest Bus Station: Bus stop outside the Centre
Car Parking: Available on site
Coach Parking: Available
Food & Drinks: Available in the Garden Centre

SPECIAL INFORMATION

The Railway operates a line at the Van Hage Garden Centre in Great Amwell. The railway is run by volunteers and any profits are donated to the local special needs school and other local charities.

OPERATING INFORMATION

Opening Times: Weekends and Bank Holidays throughout the year. Also open Tuesdays and Thursdays during the school holidays. Usually open from 11.00am to 5.00pm but from 11.00am to 4.30pm on Sundays.
Steam Working: Most operating days.
Prices: 80p per person per ride. Under-2s travel free of charge.

Detailed Directions by Car:
From the South: Take the A10 towards Cambridge and exit at the first Ware junction signposted for A414. Take the 2nd exit at the roundabout onto the A1170 towards Ware and Van Hage Garden Centre is on the left after 600 metres; From the East: Take the A414 from Harlow and turn off onto the A1170 for Ware. Then as above.

EAST KENT RAILWAY

Address: Station Road, Shepherdswell, Dover, Kent CT15 7PD	**Nº of Steam Locos**: 1
Telephone Nº: (01304) 832042	**Nº of Other Locos**: 7 + 2 DMUs
Year Formed: 1985	**Nº of Members**: 400
Location of Line: Between Shepherdswell and Eythorne	**Annual Membership Fee**: £15.00 (Adult)
Length of Line: 2 miles	**Approx Nº of Visitors P.A.**: 4,500
	Gauge: Standard and also 5 inch and 3¼ inch miniature gauges
	Web site: www.eastkentrailway.co.uk

GENERAL INFORMATION

Nearest Mainline Station: Shepherdswell (50 yards)
Car Parking: Available Shepherdswell and Eythorne
Coach Parking: In adjacent Station Yard
Souvenir Shop(s): Yes
Food & Drinks: Yes

SPECIAL INFORMATION

The East Kent Railway was originally built between 1911 and 1917 to service Tilmanstone Colliery. Closed in the mid-1980's, the railway was re-opened in 1995.

OPERATING INFORMATION

Opening Times: The 2010 operating season has a special 'Travel for a Pound' day on 21st March and then runs from 2nd April until 19th September. Trains run every Sunday and Bank Holiday during this period plus Saturdays in August and during some special events including Halloween and Santa Specials. Contact the railway for further details.
Steam Working: None at present.
Prices: Adult £7.00
Child £4.00
Senior Citizens £6.00
Family £17.00 (2 Adults and 2 Children)

Detailed Directions by Car:
From the A2: Take the turning to Shepherdswell and continue to the village. Pass the shop on the left and cross the railway bridge. Take the next left (Station Road) signposted at the traffic lights for the EKR; From the A256: Take the turning for Eythorne at the roundabout on the section between Eastry and Whitfield. Follow the road through Eythorne. Further on you will cross the railway line and enter Shepherdswell. After a few hundred yards take the right turn signposted for the EKR.

EASTLEIGH LAKESIDE STEAM RAILWAY

Address: Lakeside Country Park, Wide Lane, Eastleigh, Hants. SO50 5PE	**Nº of Steam Locos:** 18
Telephone Nº: (023) 8061-2020	**Nº of Other Locos:** 3
Year Formed: 1992	**Nº of Members:** –
Location: Opposite Southampton airport	**Approx Nº of Visitors P.A.:** 50,000
Length of Line: 1¼ miles	**Gauge:** 10¼ inches and 7¼ inches
	Web site: www.steamtrain.co.uk

GENERAL INFORMATION

Nearest Mainline Station: Southampton Airport (Parkway) (¼ mile)
Nearest Bus Station: Eastleigh (1½ miles)
Car Parking: Free parking available on site
Coach Parking: Free parking available on site
Souvenir Shop(s): Yes
Food & Drinks: Cafe on site when railway is open

SPECIAL INFORMATION

The railway also has a playground and picnic area overlooking the lakes.

OPERATING INFORMATION

Opening Times: Weekends throughout the year and daily from mid-July until mid-September plus all other school holidays. Open 10.00am to 4.30pm (until 4.00pm during the winter months). Santa Specials run on some dates in December.
Steam Working: As above
Prices: Adult Return £3.00 (First Class £3.50)
Child Return £2.50 (First Class £3.00)
Tickets are available offering 3 return journeys at reduced rates. Annual season tickets are available. Children under the age of 2 years ride free of charge. Driver training courses can be booked in advance.

Detailed Directions by Car:
From All Parts: Exit the M27 at Junction 5 and take the A335 to Eastleigh. The Railway is situated ¼ mile past Southampton Airport Station on the left hand side of the A335.

EPPING ONGAR RAILWAY

Address: Ongar Station, Ongar, Essex, CM5 9BN	**Nº of Steam Locos**: 5 (None in steam)
Telephone Nº: (01277) 365200	**Nº of Other Locos**: 4
Year Formed: 2004	**Nº of Members**: 120
Location of Line: Epping to Ongar	**Annual Membership Fee**: –
Length of Line: 6 miles	**Approx Nº of Visitors P.A.**: 6,000
	Gauge: Standard gauge and also 5 feet
	Web site: www.eorailway.co.uk

GENERAL INFORMATION

Nearest Mainline Station: Epping L.U.L. (6½ miles from Ongar Station)
Nearest Bus Station: Epping (6½ miles)
Car Parking: Limited free parking at Ongar and North Weald stations.
Coach Parking: By arrangement only
Souvenir Shop(s): Yes
Food & Drinks: Available

SPECIAL INFORMATION

The Railway has 5 Finnish locomotives on display which unfortunately are not able to use the line due to their 5 foot gauge.

OPERATING INFORMATION

The railway is currently closed due to engineering and remodelling work designed to upgrade the infrastructure and safeguard the future of the line. Volunteers from the Epping Ongar Railway Society are continuing with this work in the hope that services will be able to run again later in 2010. Please check the web site for the latest news.

Detailed Directions by Car:
For North Weald Station: Exit the M11 at Junction 7 and follow the A414 towards Chelmsford and North Weald. Take the 3rd exit at the 2nd roundabout ('The Talbot' pub on the left) and follow the road into North Weald village. Station Road is on the left just after leaving the village. For Ongar Station: Exit the M11 at Junction 7 and follow the A414 towards Chelmsford and North Weald. Follow the road for approximately 5 miles going straight on at two roundabouts. At the 3rd roundabout (BP garage on the left) take the third exit towards Ongar. Epping Ongar Railway is located approximately on the right hand side after approximately 400 yards.

EXBURY GARDENS RAILWAY

Address: Exbury Gardens, Exbury,
Near Southampton   SO45 1AZ
Telephone N°: (02380) 891203
Year Formed: 2001
Location of Line: Exbury
Length of Line: 1½ miles

N° of Steam Locos: 3
N° of Other Locos: 1
N° of Members: None
Approx N° of Visitors P.A.: 55,000
Gauge: 12¼ inches
Web site: www.exbury.co.uk

GENERAL INFORMATION

Nearest Mainline Station: Brockenhurst (8 miles)
Nearest Bus Station: Hill Top (2½ miles)
Car Parking: Free parking available on site
Coach Parking: Free parking available on site
Souvenir Shop(s): Yes
Food & Drinks: Available

SPECIAL INFORMATION

The railway is located in the world famous Rothschild
azalea and rhododendron gardens at Exbury in the
New Forest. A walk-through exhibition is scheduled
to open during the Spring of 2010.

OPERATING INFORMATION

Opening Times: 2010 dates: Daily from the 13th
March to 7th November. Also open for Santa
Specials on 11th, 12th, 18th, 19th, 20th & 21st
December. Open from 10.00am to 5.00pm (or dusk
if earlier).
Steam Working: Most running days from 11.00am
(restricted operation in March and September).
Prices: Adult Return £3.50
                Child Return £3.50
Note: Day Rover tickets are available during the low
season for an additional £1.00 charge.

Detailed Directions by Car:
From all directions: Exit the M27 at Junction 2 and take the A326 to Dibden. Follow the brown tourist signs for
Exbury Gardens & Steam Railway.

FANCOTT MINIATURE RAILWAY

Address: Fancott Miniature Railway, Fancott, near Toddington, Bedfordshire
Telephone Nº: 07917 756237
Year Formed: 1996
Location of Line: The Fancott Pub, near Toddington, Bedfordshire
Length of Line: ¼ mile

Nº of Steam Locos: 0
Nº of Other Locos: 3
Approx Nº of Visitors P.A.: 10,000
Gauge: 7¼ inches
Web site: www.fancottrailway.tk
E-mail: thefmr@live.co.uk

GENERAL INFORMATION

Nearest Mainline Station: Harlington/Leagrave
Nearest Bus Station: Luton
Car Parking: 50 spaces available on site
Coach Parking: Available but no special space
Souvenir Shop(s): No
Food & Drinks: Pub/Restaurant on site

SPECIAL INFORMATION

The Railway runs through the grounds of The Fancott Pub, a former winner of the Whitbread Family Pub of the Year.

OPERATING INFORMATION

Opening Times: Open between Mothers Day and 31st September on Saturdays, Sundays and Bank Holidays from 1.00pm to dusk (6.00pm on Sundays). Also open from Tuesday to Friday during the School Holidays, 1.00pm to 5.00pm.
Steam Working: Steam locos visit on a regular basis – please contact the railway for further details.
Prices: £1.00 Adults and Children

Detailed Directions by Car:
From All Parts: Exit the M1 at Junction 12 and travel towards Toddington. After approximately 100 yards, take the B579 towards Chalton and Fancott. The Fancott pub is on the left after the second bend.

FAVERSHAM MINIATURE RAILWAY

Address: Brogdale Farm, Brogdale Road, Faversham, Kent
Telephone Nº: (01795) 474211
Year Formed: 1984
Location of Line: Faversham, Kent
Length of Line: ½ mile at present
Gauge: 9 inches

Nº of Steam Locos: 2
Nº of Other Locos: 9
Nº of Members: 40
Annual Membership Fee: £10.00 Adult, £25.00 Family
Approx Nº of Visitors P.A.: 3,500
Web site: www.fmrs.org.uk

GENERAL INFORMATION

Nearest Mainline Station: Faversham (¾ mile)
Nearest Bus Station: None, but a regular bus service travels to Faversham from Canterbury
Car Parking: Available on site
Coach Parking: Available on site
Souvenir Shop(s): Various shops on site
Food & Drinks: Available

SPECIAL INFORMATION

Faversham Miniature Railway is the only 9 inch gauge railway open to the public in the UK.

OPERATING INFORMATION

Opening Times: Sundays and Bank Holiday weekends from March to November.
Steam Working: Special steam days only. Please contact the Railway for further details.
Prices: £1.00 per ride

Detailed Directions by Car:
Exit the M2 at Junction 5 and take the A251 towards Faversham. After about ½ mile turn left onto the A2 then left again after ¼ mile turning into Brogdale Road for the Farm and Railway.

FRIMLEY LODGE MINIATURE RAILWAY

Address: Frimley Lodge Park, Sturt Road, Frimley Green, Surrey   GU16 6HT
Phone Nº: 07710 606461 (Please use on operating days only)
Year Formed: 1991
Location of Line: Frimley Green
Length of Line: 1 kilometre

Nº of Steam Locos: 5 (Members' locos)
Nº of Other Locos: 3
Nº of Members: Approximately 60
Approx Nº of Visitors P.A.: 20,000+
Gauge: 3½ inches, 5 inches & 7¼ inches
Web site: www.flmr.org

GENERAL INFORMATION

Nearest Mainline Station: Frimley or Ashvale (both 2 miles)
Nearest Bus Station: Farnborough (4 miles) – No buses on a Sunday however!
Car Parking: Available on site
Coach Parking: Available by prior arrangement
Food & Drinks: Cafe in the Park

SPECIAL INFORMATION

The Railway is operated by volunteers from the Frimley and Ascot Locomotive Club who bring their own Locomotives to give pleasure to others. All the proceeds are used for the maintenance of the Railway and to benefit local charities.

OPERATING INFORMATION

Opening Times: The first Sunday of the month from March to November. Also on August Bank Holiday and Wednesdays during the school holidays (subject to staff availability). Trains run from 11.00am to 5.00pm on Sundays and from 11.00am – 1.00pm then 2.00pm – 4.00pm when open on Wednesdays.
Steam Working: Operational Sundays only.
Prices: Single Rides £1.00
        Double Rides £1.20

Detailed Directions by Car:
Exit the M3 at Junction 4 and take the A331 towards Guildford. Leave the A331 at the turn-off for Mytchett and turn left at the top of the ramp then left again at the Miners Arms into Sturt Road. Cross over the bridge then turn right into Frimley Lodge Park. Once in the Park turn right then right again then take the next left for the Railway.

GOFFS PARK LIGHT RAILWAY

Correspondence: c/o 8 Le May Close, Horley, Surrey   RH6 7JH
Telephone Nº: None
Year Formed: 1958
Location of Line: Goffs Park, Crawley
Length of Line: 1,200 feet

Nº of Steam Locos: 15
Nº of Other Locos: 6
Nº of Members: Approximately 30
Approx Nº of Visitors P.A.: 5,000
Gauge: 3½ inches and 5 inches

GENERAL INFORMATION

Nearest Mainline Station: Crawley (½ mile)
Nearest Bus Station: Crawley (½ mile)
Car Parking: Limited parking available on site
Coach Parking: None
Food & Drinks: None

OPERATING INFORMATION

Opening Times: Sundays and Bank Holidays from Easter to October. Trains run from 2.00pm to 5.00pm.
Steam Working: Most operating days.
Prices: 30p per ride.

Detailed Directions by Car:
Goffs Park is located near the centre of Crawley in Horsham Road (the A2220), adjacent to the level crossing with the mainline railway.

GOLDING SPRING MINIATURE RAILWAY

Address: Quainton Road Station, Quainton, Aylesbury, Bucks. HP22 4BY **Phone Nº:** (01296) 623540 (Secretary) **Year Formed:** 1972 **Location:** Within the Buckinghamshire Railway Centre site **Length of Line:** 1,200 yards	**Nº of Steam Locos:** 12 **Nº of Other Locos:** 4 **Nº of Members:** Approximately 120 **Approx Nº of Visitors P.A.:** 25,000 **Gauge:** 3½ inches, 5 inches & 7¼ inches **Web site:** www.vames.co.uk

GENERAL INFORMATION

Nearest Mainline Station: Aylesbury (6 miles)
Nearest Bus Station: Aylesbury (6 miles)
Car Parking: Free parking for 500 cars available
Coach Parking: Free parking for 10 coaches
Souvenir Shop(s): Yes
Food & Drinks: Yes

SPECIAL INFORMATION

The Golding Spring Miniature Railway is operated by members of the Vale of Aylesbury Model Engineering Society and is located at the Buckinghamshire Railway Centre. Other attractions include a 32mm and 45mm Garden Railway.

OPERATING INFORMATION

Opening Times: Sundays and Bank Holidays from March to October inclusive. Also on Wednesdays in the school holidays to coincide with the Bucks Railway Centre. Trains run from 10.30am to 4.30pm
Steam Working: Every operational day.
Prices: 80p per ride
          Under-3s travel free of charge

Detailed Directions by Car:
The Buckinghamshire Railway Centre is signposted off the A41 Aylesbury to Bicester Road at Waddesdon and off the A413 Buckingham to Aylesbury road at Whitchurch. Junctions 7, 8 and 9 of the M40 are all close by.

GREAT COCKCROW RAILWAY

Address: Hardwick Lane, Lyne, near Chertsey, Surrey KT16 0AD	**N° of Steam Locos**: Approximately 25
Telephone N°: (01932) 565474 (Sundays)	**N° of Other Locos**: 3
Year Formed: 1968	**Approx N° of Visitors P.A.**: 10,000
Location of Line: Lyne, near Chertsey	**Gauge**: 7¼ inches
Length of Line: 2 miles	**Web site**: www.cockcrow.co.uk

GENERAL INFORMATION

Nearest Mainline Station: Chertsey (30 min. walk)
Nearest Bus Stop: Chertsey (30 minute walk)
Car Parking: Available on site
Coach Parking: Limited parking available on site
Souvenir Shop(s): None
Food & Drinks: Available

SPECIAL INFORMATION

Emanating from the Greywood Central Railway, built from 1946, at a private address in Walton-on-Thames, the Great Cockcrow Railway opened in 1968 and has continually grown since moving to its present site. The Railway offers a choice of two regular routes, each served every few minutes.

OPERATING INFORMATION

Opening Times: 2010 dates: Sundays from 2nd May to 24th October when trains run from 2.00pm to 5.00pm. Also open on Wednesdays in August (12.00pm to 4.00pm) and on 30th October (5.00pm to 8.00pm).
Steam Working: Every operating day.
Prices: Various combinations of tickets are available ranging from £3.00 for an ordinary adult return to £15.00 for a family double return.

Detailed Directions by Car:
Exit the M25 at Junction 11 and take the A320 towards Woking. At the first roundabout take the exit towards Chertsey and continue along this road passing St. Peter's Hospital on the left, then turn next left (B386) towards Windlesham. Turn right almost immediately into Hardwick Lane and the railway on the right after about ¼ mile just after Hardwick Farm.   Satellite Navigation: KT16 0AD

GREAT WHIPSNADE RAILWAY

Address: ZSL Whipsnade Zoo, Dunstable LU6 2LF	**Nº of Steam Locos:** 2
Telephone Nº: (01582) 872171	**Nº of Other Locos:** 5
Year Formed: 1970	**Nº of Members:** None
Location of Line: ZSL Whipsnade Zoo, Near Dunstable	**Approx Nº of Visitors P.A.:** 130,000
Length of Line: 1¾ miles	**Gauge:** 2 feet 6 inches
	Web site: www.zsl.org

GENERAL INFORMATION

Nearest Mainline Station: Luton (7 miles)
Nearest Bus Station: Dunstable (3 miles)
Car Parking: Available just outside the park
Coach Parking: Available just outside the park
Souvenir Shop(s): Next to the Station
Food & Drinks: Available

SPECIAL INFORMATION

The Railway is situated in the ZSL Whipsnade Zoo operated by the Zoological Society of London.

OPERATING INFORMATION

Opening Times: The zoo is open daily from 10.00am throughout the year. Closing time varies from 4.00pm to 6.00pm depending on the time of the year. The railway runs daily from 31st March until 28th October and at weekends at some other times of the year. Contact the zoo for further details.
Steam Working: Every operating day.
Prices: Adult £18.50
           Child £14.50
           Family Ticket £60.00
           Senior Citizen £17.00
Note: The above prices are for entrance into the Zoo itself. Train rides are an additional charge for adults but free for children. The prices shown above include a £1.80 voluntary donation.

Detailed Directions by Car:
From All Parts: Exit the M1 at Junction 11 and take the A505 then the B489. Follow signs for Whipsnade Zoo.

GREAT WOBURN RAILWAY

Address: Woburn Safari Park MK17 9QN	**Nº of Steam Locos**: None
Telephone Nº: (01525) 290407	**Nº of Other Locos**: 3
Year Formed: 1970	**Approx Nº of Visitors P.A.**: Over 420,000
Location of Line: Near Milton Keynes	(to the Park)
Length of Line: 1½ miles	**Gauge**: 2 feet 6 inches
	Web site: www.woburn.co.uk

GENERAL INFORMATION

Nearest Mainline Station: Ridgmont (1½ miles)
Nearest Tube Station: Milton Keynes (11 miles)
Car Parking: Available on site
Coach Parking: Available on site
Souvenir Shop(s): Yes
Food & Drinks: Available

SPECIAL INFORMATION

The railway runs around Woburn Safari Park which
also houses a number of other attractions.

OPERATING INFORMATION

Opening Times: Daily from the beginning of
March to the end of October from 10.00am to
5.00pm. Weekends only from mid-November to the
end of February, 11.00am to 3.00pm.
Steam Working: None
Prices: Adults £18.50 (Admission to the park)
Children £13.50 (Admission to the park)
Concessions £15.50 (Admission to park)
Family £52.00 (Admission to the park)
Note: Prices are reduced during the Winter months.

Detailed Directions by Car:
From All Parts: Exit the M1 at Junction 13 and take the A507 then the A4012 to Woburn Safari Park which is
clearly signposted.

GUILDFORD M.E.S. RAILWAY

Address: Burchatts Farm, Stoke Park, Guildford, Surrey GU1 1TU	**Nº of Steam Locos:** 6 + visiting locos
Telephone Nº: None	**Nº of Other Locos:** 1
Year Formed: 1954	**Nº of Members:** Over 200
Location of Line: Stoke Park, Guildford	**Approx Nº of Visitors P.A.:** 7,000
Length of Line: 990 feet ground level track and 1,405 feet raised track	**Gauges:** 7¼ inches, 5 inches, 3½ inches and 2½ inches
	Web site: www.gmes.org.uk

GENERAL INFO

Nearest Mainline Station:
Guildford London Road (½ mile)
Nearest Bus Station:
Guildford (2½ miles)
Car Parking: Street parking + some available on site
Coach Parking:
Street parking only
Souvenir Shop(s): None
Food & Drinks: Available

SPECIAL INFO

The Guildford Model Engineering Society has operated a railway at the Burchatts Farm site since 1958 and a 'Garden railway' also operates on site.

OPERATING INFO

Opening Times:
2010 Dates: 18th April, 23rd May, 20th June, 15th August and 19th September – open from 2.00pm to 5.00pm on these dates. Open on 10th October 1.00pm to 4.00pm. Also open for a Model Steam Rally and Exhibition on 10th & 11th July from 11.00am to 5.00pm.
Steam Working: Every open day.
Prices: 50p per ride on normal open days.
Admission prices for the Steam
Rally: Adults £7.00
          Children – Free of charge
          Senior Citizens £6.00

Detailed Directions by Car:
The Railway is located at the Eastern end of Stoke Park in Guildford, not far from the Spectrum Sports Centre and near to the junction of the A25 (Parkway) and the A3100 (London Road). Access to the Burchatts Farm site is via London Road.

HARLINGTON LOCOMOTIVE SOCIETY

Address: High Street, Harlington, Hayes, Middlesex   UB3 5DF
Telephone Nº: None
Year Formed: 1947
Location of Line: Harlington High Street
Length of Line: 1,047 feet

Nº of Steam Locos: 40 (Members' locos)
Nº of Other Locos: Several
Nº of Members: Approximately 65
Approx Nº of Visitors P.A.: 3,000
Gauge: 3½ inches and 5 inches
Web site: www.harlingtonlocomotivesociety.org.uk

GENERAL INFORMATION

Nearest Mainline Station: Hayes (1½ miles)
Nearest Bus Stop: 50 yards – Services 90, H98 & 140
Car Parking: Limited on site parking. Also street parking available.
Coach Parking: None
Food & Drinks: Light refreshments are available

SPECIAL INFORMATION

Approximately 40 Steam plus several Electric locos are owned by individual members. Typically 4 locos will be in steam on most open days.

OPERATING INFORMATION

Opening Times: The 2nd & 4th Sundays of each month from Easter until October. 2.00pm to 5.00pm. Also open for Birthday parties and Santa Specials.
Steam Working: Every operating day.
Prices: 40p per ride (Under-3s accompanied by a paying adult ride free of charge).

Detailed Directions by Car:
Exit the M25 at Junction 14, initially following signs for Heathrow. At the first roundabout, turn left onto the A3044 towards the A4, passing the new Terminal 5 building on the right hand side. On reaching the A4 turn right towards London. After 2½ miles, at Harlington Corner, turn left onto the A437. The Railway is situated in Harlington village centre on the right, approximately 75 yards after crossing over the mini-roundabout.

HAYLING SEASIDE RAILWAY

Address: Beachlands, Sea Front Road, Hayling Island, Hampshire   PO11 0AG
Telephone Nº: (02392) 372427
Year Formed: 2001
Location: Beachlands to Eastoke Corner
Length of Line: 1 mile
Web site: www.haylingseasiderailway.co.uk

Nº of Steam Locos: Visiting locos only
Nº of Other Locos: 4
Nº of Members: Approximately 100
Annual Membership Fee: £10.00
Approx Nº of Visitors P.A.: 25,000
Gauge: 2 feet

GENERAL INFORMATION

Nearest Mainline Station: Havant
Nearest Bus Station: Beachlands
Car Parking: Spaces are available at both Beachlands and Eastoke Corner.
Coach Parking: Beachlands and Eastoke Corner
Souvenir Shop(s): Yes
Food & Drinks: Available

SPECIAL INFORMATION

The Railway runs along Hayling Island beach front where there are fantastic views across the Solent to the Isle of Wight.

OPERATING INFORMATION

Opening Times: Every Saturday, Sunday and Wednesday throughout the year and daily during the School holidays. Various specials run at different times of the year – please check the web site or phone the Railway for further details. The first train normally departs at 11.00am from Beachlands.
Steam Working: Visiting locos only. Please contact the railway for further information.
Prices: Adult Return £3.50
         Child/Senior Citizen Return £2.00
         Family Return £7.00 (2 Adult + 2 Child)
         Dogs travel free of charge!

Detailed Directions by Car:
Exit the A27 at Havant Roundabout and proceed to Hayling Island and Beachlands Station following the road signs. Parking is available south of the Carousel Amusement Park. Beachlands Station is within the car park.

HOLLYCOMBE STEAM COLLECTION

Address: Hollycombe, Liphook, Hants. GU30 7LP	**Nº of Steam Locos**: 6
Telephone Nº: (01428) 724900	**Nº of Other Locos**: 2
Year Formed: 1970	**Nº of Members**: 100
Location of Line: Hollycombe, Liphook	**Annual Membership Fee**: £8.00
Length of Line: 1¾ miles Narrow gauge, ¼ mile Standard gauge	**Approx Nº of Visitors P.A.**: 35,000
	Gauge: 2 feet plus Standard & 7¼ inches
	Web site: www.hollycombe.co.uk

GENERAL INFORMATION

Nearest Mainline Station: Liphook (1 mile)
Nearest Bus Station: Liphook
Car Parking: Extensive grass area
Coach Parking: Hardstanding
Souvenir Shop(s): Yes
Food & Drinks: Yes – Cafe

SPECIAL INFORMATION

The narrow gauge railway ascends to spectacular views of the Downs and is part of an extensive working steam museum.

OPERATING INFORMATION

Opening Times: 2010 dates: Sundays and Bank Holidays from Easter until the 24th October. Also open Tuesday to Friday in August.
Steam Working: The Standard Gauge steam weekend is held at the start of June 2010 and features a Belgian vertical boiler tank Locomotive. Please contact the railway for further information.
Prices: Adult £11.00
Child £9.00
Senior Citizen £9.00
Family £35.00 (2 adults + 3 children)

Detailed Directions by Car:
Take the A3 to Liphook and follow the brown tourist signs for the railway.

HOTHAM PARK MINIATURE RAILWAY

Address: Hotham Park, Bognor Regis, PO21 1HR
Telephone Nº: (01638) 741084
Year Formed: 2007
Location of Line: Bognor Regis
Length of Line: 900 yards

Nº of Steam Locos: None
Nº of Other Locos: 1
Nº of Members: –
Approx Nº of Visitors P.A.: 20,000
Gauge: 12¼ inches
Web site: www.hothamparkrailway.co.uk

GENERAL INFORMATION

Nearest Mainline Station: Bognor Regis (¼ mile)
Nearest Bus Station: Bognor Regis (½ mile)
Car Parking: Available on site
Coach Parking: Available
Souvenir Shop(s): None
Food & Drinks: None

SPECIAL INFORMATION

The railway is located in Hotham Park, a recently restored 18th Century Park situated in the heart of Bognor Regis.

OPERATING INFORMATION

Opening Times: Weekends throughout the year and daily during School Holidays, weather permitting. Trains run from 10.00am to 5.00pm.
Steam Working: None at present.
Prices: Adults £2.00
    Children £1.50
    Supersaver card £10.00 for 8 rides

Detailed Directions by Car:
From All Parts: Hotham Park is situated by the side of the A259 across the top end of Bognor Regis High Street and opposite Butlins.

HYTHE FERRY PIER RAILWAY

Address: Hythe Ferry Pier, Prospect Place, Hythe   SO45 6AU
Telephone Nº: (023) 8084-0722
Year Formed: Installed 1921
Location of Line: Hythe Pier
Length of Line: 600 metres

Nº of Steam Locos: None
Nº of Other Locos: 2
Nº of Members: –
Approx Nº of Visitors P.A.: 500,000
Gauge: 2 feet
Web site: www.hytheferry.co.uk

GENERAL INFORMATION

Nearest Mainline Station: Southampton (2 miles)
Nearest Bus Station: Southampton (2 miles)
Car Parking: Paid parking nearby
Coach Parking: Paid parking nearby
Souvenir Shop(s): Yes – nearby
Food & Drinks: Yes – nearby

SPECIAL INFORMATION

The railway operates along a Victorian Pier and takes passengers to a ferry which operates a regular half-hourly service crossing the harbour from Hythe to Southampton. This is the world's oldest continually working pier train.

OPERATING INFORMATION

Opening Times: The ferry and therefore railway operates daily. The first ferry departs Hythe at 6.10am on weekdays and 7.10am on Saturdays. Sundays and Bank Holidays run from 9.40am to 6.00pm.
Prices: Pier Entrance fee £1.00 (included in the cost of a Ferry ticket)
Note: Ferry fares are an additional charge and vary depending whether they are peak or off-peak.

Detailed Directions by Car:
Hythe Ferry Pier is located by the waterside in Hythe adjacent to the Promenade and the Marina.

ICKENHAM MINIATURE RAILWAY

Correspondence: 25 Copthall Road East, Ickenham, Middlesex UB10 8SD	**Nº of Steam Locos**: Up to 6
Telephone Nº: (01895) 630125	**Nº of Other Locos**: Up to 6
Year Formed: 1948	**Nº of Members**: Approximately 70
Location: At the rear of the "Coach and Horses" Public House, Ickenham	**Approx Nº of Visitors P.A.**: 9,000
Length of Line: 1,100 feet	**Gauge**: 3½ inches and 5 inches
	Web site: www.idsme.co.uk

GENERAL INFORMATION

Nearest Mainline Station: West Ruislip (½ mile)
Nearest Underground Station: Ickenham (¼ mile)
Car Parking: Public car park is adjacent
Coach Parking: None
Food & Drinks: Available

SPECIAL INFORMATION

The Railway is operated by volunteers from the Ickenham & District Society of Model Engineers.

OPERATING INFORMATION

Opening Times: The first Saturday of the month from April to December inclusive. Trains run from 12.00pm to 5.30pm (or until dusk later in the year).
Steam Working: All operating days subject to availability.
Prices: 40p per ride.

Detailed Directions by Car:
The Railway is located in Ickenham Village behind the Coach and Horses Public House which is adjacent to the junction of the B466 Ickenham High Road, B466 Long Lane and the B467 Swakeleys Road. From the East: Exit the A40 at Hillingdon Circus turning right onto the B466 Long Lane towards Ickenham/Ruislip. Continue for 1 mile and turn right into Community Close for the car park just before the Coach and Horses in the centre of Ickenham; From the West: Exit the A40 at Hillingdon Circus turning left onto B466 Long Lane. Then as above.

ILFORD & WEST ESSEX MODEL RAILWAY CLUB

Address: Station Road, Chadwell Heath, Romford, Essex	**N⁰ of Steam Locos**: 3
Telephone N⁰: (01708) 450424	**N⁰ of Other Locos**: 2
Year Formed: 1930	**N⁰ of Members**: Approximately 50
Location of Line: Chadwell Heath	**Approx N⁰ of Visitors P.A.**: 400
Length of Line: 150 yards	**Gauge**: 7¼ inches
	Web site: www.iwemrc.org.uk

GENERAL INFORMATION

Nearest Mainline Station: Chadwell Heath
Nearest Bus Station: Chadwell Heath (100 yards)
Car Parking: None on site but a public car park is 100 yards away
Coach Parking: None
Food & Drinks: Light refreshments are available

SPECIAL INFORMATION

The Ilford & West Essex Model Railway Club was formed in 1930 and as such is one of the oldest clubs of its type in the country. Please note that access to the site is by steps only and it is therefore not suitable for wheelchairs.

OPERATING INFORMATION

Opening Times: The first Sunday of the month from April to September inclusive. Trains run from 10.30am to 4.00pm.
Steam Working: All operating days.
Prices: 50p per ride

Detailed Directions by Car:
The site is alongside Chadwell Heath mainline station just off the A118 between Romford and Ilford town centres. Station Road is to the South of the A118 approximately half-way between the two towns. The site itself is approximately 200 yards down Station Road with a car park on the right hand side.

ISLE OF WIGHT STEAM RAILWAY

Address: The Railway Station, Haven Street, Ryde, Isle of Wight   PO33 4DS
Telephone No: (01983) 882204
Year Formed: 1971 (re-opened)
Location: Smallbrook Junction to Wootton
Length of Line: 5 miles
No of Steam Locos: 11

No of Other Locos: 3
No of Members: 1,300
Annual Membership Fee: £20.00
Approx No of Visitors P.A.: 100,000
Gauge: Standard
Talking Timetable: (01983) 884343
Web site: www.iwsteamrailway.co.uk

GENERAL INFORMATION

Nearest Mainline Station: Smallbrook Junction (direct interchange)
Nearest Bus: From Ryde & Newport direct
Car Parking: Free parking at Havenstreet & Wootton Stations
Coach Parking: Free at Havenstreet Station
Souvenir Shop(s): Yes – at Havenstreet Station
Food & Drinks: Yes – at Havenstreet Station

SPECIAL INFORMATION

The IWSR uses mostly Victorian & Edwardian locomotives and carriages to recreate the atmosphere of an Isle of Wight branch line railway.

OPERATING INFORMATION

Opening Times: Selected dates between March and December and also daily from mid-June to mid-September. Please contact the railway for further information.
Steam Working: 10.30am to 4.00pm (depending on the Station)
Prices: Adult Return £9.00
          Child Return £5.00
          Family Return £24.00
               (2 adults + 2 children)

Detailed Directions by Car:
To reach the Isle of Wight head for the Ferry ports at Lymington, Southampton or Portsmouth. From all parts of the Isle of Wight, head for Ryde and follow the brown tourist signs.

KENT & EAST SUSSEX RAILWAY

Address: Tenterden Town Station, Tenterden, Kent TN30 6HE	**Nº of Steam Locos:** 12
Telephone Nº: (01580) 765155	**Nº of Other Locos:** 6
Year Formed: 1974	**Nº of Members:** 2,100
Location of Line: Tenterden, Kent to Bodiam, East Sussex	**Annual Membership Fee:** £23.00
	Approx Nº of Visitors P.A.: 99,000
	Gauge: Standard
Length of Line: 10½ miles	**Web site:** www.kesr.org.uk

GENERAL INFORMATION

Nearest Mainline Station: Headcorn (8 miles)
Nearest Bus Station: Tenterden
Car Parking: Free parking available at Tenterden Town and Northiam Stations
Coach Parking: Tenterden & Northiam
Souvenir Shop(s): Yes
Food & Drinks: Yes

SPECIAL INFORMATION

Built as Britain's first light railway, the K&ESR opened in 1900 and was epitomised by sharp curved and steep gradients and to this day retains a charm and atmosphere all of its own.

OPERATING INFORMATION

Opening Times: From March to October and in December. The return journey time is 1 hour 55 minutes. Please phone the 24 hour talking-timetable for precise operating information: (01580) 762943
Steam Working: Every operational day
Prices: Adult Ticket – £12.80
Child Ticket – £7.80
Senior Citizen Ticket – £11.80
Family Ticket – £34.00
(2 adults + 3 children or 1 adult + 4 children)
Note: The prices shown above are for Day Rover tickets which allow unlimited travel on the day of purchase.

Detailed Directions by Car:
From London and Kent Coast: Travel to Ashford (M20) then take the A28 to Tenterden; From Sussex Coast: Take A28 from Hastings to Northiam.

KNEBWORTH PARK MINIATURE RAILWAY

Address: c/o Estate Office, Knebworth, Hertfordshire   SG3 6PY
Telephone Nº: (01438) 812661
Year Formed: 1991 (Miniature Railway)
Location of Line: Knebworth Park
Length of Line: 800 yards

Nº of Steam Locos: One
Nº of Other Locos: 6
Nº of Members: None
Approx Nº of Visitors P.A.: 35,000
Gauge: 10¼ inches
Web site: www.knebworthrailway.co.nr

GENERAL INFORMATION

Nearest Mainline Station: Knebworth
Nearest Bus Station: Stevenage
Car Parking: Available on site
Coach Parking: Available on site
Souvenir Shop(s): Yes
Food & Drinks: Yes

SPECIAL INFORMATION

The Railway is located in the grounds of the historic Knebworth House.

OPERATING INFORMATION

Opening Times: 2010 dates: Daily from 2nd to 18th April, 29th May to 6th June then 3rd July to 31st August. Closed on 31st July to 3rd August. Open on weekends and Bank Holidays only from 24th April to 23rd May, 12th to 27th June and 4th to 26th September inclusive. Trains run from 12.00pm to 5.00pm on these dates.
Steam Working: Please contact the railway for further details.
Prices: Adult £7.50 – £9.50
Child/Senior Citizen £7.50–£9.00
Family Ticket £26.00 – £33.00
Note: Prices shown above are for entrance into Knebworth Park and House. One free train ride is included with the entrance fee. Subsequent rides are charged as follows:
Adult £1.90   Child £1.60

Detailed Directions by Car:
From All Parts: Exit the A1(M) at Junction 7 and follow signs for Knebworth Park. After entering the Park, follow signs for the Adventure Playground for the Railway.

LANGFORD & BEELEIGH RAILWAY

Address: Museum of Power, Hatfield Road, Langford, Maldon, Essex, CM9 6QA	**N⁰ of Steam Locos:** 4
	N⁰ of Other Locos: 1
	N⁰ of Members: Approximately 160
Telephone N⁰: (01621) 843183	**Approx N⁰ of Visitors P.A.:** 6,000
Year Formed: 1999	**Gauge:** 7¼ inches
Length of Line: ¼ mile loop	**Web site:** www.museumofpower.org.uk

GENERAL INFORMATION

Nearest Mainline Station: Witham (4 miles)
Nearest Bus Station: Chelmsford (6 miles)
Car Parking: Available on site
Coach Parking: Available
Souvenir Shop(s): Yes
Food & Drinks: Available

SPECIAL INFORMATION

The Railway is situated at the Museum of Power which is housed in the Steam Pumping Station at Langford in Essex. The Museum was set up to exhibit and demonstrate working examples of power sources of all types and chronicle the major roles that they have played in history.

OPERATING INFORMATION

Opening Times: Trains run on the first Sunday of the month from April to October inclusive and also during Special events at various times of the year. Please contact the Museum for further information.
Steam Working: On all operating days.
Prices: £1.00 per ride.
Note: Admission to the Museum is an extra charge.

Detailed Directions by Car:
The Museum is situated in Langford, on the B1019 Maldon to Hatfield Peverel Road. From the A12, take the Hatfield Peverel exit, pass through the village and take the B1019 Hatfield Road towards Ulting & Maldon. The Museum is on the right hand side after approximately 3 miles on the outskirts of Langford.

THE LAVENDER LINE

<table>
<tr><td>

Address: Isfield Station, Isfield, near Uckfield, East Sussex TN22 5XB
Telephone Nº: (01825) 750515
Year Formed: 1992
Location of Line: East Sussex between Lewes and Uckfield
Length of Line: 1 mile

</td><td>

Nº of Steam Locos: 1
Nº of Other Locos: 3 + DEMU
Nº of Members: Approximately 400
Annual Membership Fee: £15.00
Approx Nº of Visitors P.A.: 12,500
Gauge: Standard
Web site: www.lavender-line.co.uk

</td></tr>
</table>

GENERAL INFORMATION

Nearest Mainline Station: Uckfield (3 miles)
Nearest Bus Station: Uckfield (3 miles)
Car Parking: Free parking at site
Coach Parking: Can cater for coach parties – please contact the Railway.
Souvenir Shop: Yes
Food & Drinks: Yes – Cinders Buffet

SPECIAL INFORMATION

Isfield Station has been restored as a Southern Railway country station complete with the original L.B.S.C.R. signalbox.

OPERATING INFORMATION

Opening Times: Sundays throughout the year. Some Weekends in June, July and August plus Wednesdays and Thursdays in August. Also open on Bank Holidays, daily during February and October School half-term holidays and for Santa Specials in December.
Steam Working: Please phone for details.
Prices: Adult £8.00
Child £5.00
Senior Citizen £7.00
Family Ticket £26.00
(2 adults + 3 children)
All tickets offer unlimited rides on the day of issue and prices may vary on special event days.

Detailed Directions by Car::
From All Parts: Isfield is just off the A26 midway between Lewes and Uckfield.

LEIGHTON BUZZARD RAILWAY

Address: Pages Park Station, Billington Road, Leighton Buzzard, Beds. LU7 4TN	**N° of Steam Locos**: 12
Telephone N°: (01525) 373888	**N° of Other Locos**: 41
Year Formed: 1967	**N° of Members**: 400
Location of Line: Leighton Buzzard	**Annual Membership Fee**: £21.00
Length of Line: 3 miles	**Approx N° of Visitors P.A.**: 21,000
	Gauge: 2 feet
	Web site: www.buzzrail.co.uk

GENERAL INFORMATION

Nearest Mainline Station: Leighton Buzzard (2 miles)
Nearest Bus Station: Leighton Buzzard (¾ mile)
Car Parking: Free parking adjacent
Coach Parking: Free parking adjacent
Souvenir Shop(s): Yes
Food & Drinks: Yes

SPECIAL INFORMATION

The railway was constructed in 1919 using surplus materials from World War I battlefield supply lines. Until 1968, it was a freight-only line, servicing Stonehenge brickworks.

OPERATING INFORMATION

Opening Times: 2010 dates: Sundays from 14th March to 31st October plus Bank Holiday weekends. Also open on some Saturdays and weekdays. Trains run from mid-morning to late afternoon and Santa Specials run on some dates in December. Please contact the railway or visit their web site for further information.
Steam Working: Most operating days.
Prices: Adult £8.00
Child £4.00
Senior Citizens £6.00
Family Ticket £22.00 (2 Adult + 2 Child)
Family Ticket £18.00 (2 Adult + 1 Child)

Detailed Directions by Car:
Travel to Leighton Buzzard then follow the brown tourist signs showing a steam train. Pages Park Station is ¾ mile to the south of the Town Centre. From the A505/A4146 bypass, turn towards Leighton Buzzard at the roundabout by McDonalds, following the brown tourist signs.

LITTLEDOWN MINIATURE RAILWAY

Address: Littledown Park, Chaseside, Castle Lane East, Bournemouth, BH7 7DX
Telephone Nº: None
Year Formed: 1924
Location of Line: Littledown Park
Length of Line: Over one third of a mile

Nº of Steam Locos: 15+
Nº of Other Locos: 10+
Nº of Members: 120+
Approx Nº of Visitors P.A.: 4,000
Gauge: 3½ inches, 5 inches & 7¼ inches
Web site: www.littledownrailway.co.uk

GENERAL INFORMATION

Nearest Mainline Station: Bournemouth Central (3½ miles)
Nearest Bus Station: Bournemouth
Car Parking: In Littledown Leisure Centre car park
Coach Parking: As above

SPECIAL INFORMATION

Bournemouth and District Society of Model Engineers operate the railway at Littledown Park.

OPERATING INFORMATION

Opening Times: Most Sundays and Wednesdays throughout the year subject to weather conditions. Trains run from 11.00am to 3.00pm.
Steam Working: Subject to availability. Please contact the railway for further details.
Prices: £1.00 per ride.

Detailed Directions by Car:
The Railway is situated at Littledown Park which is to the North-East of Bournemouth town centre close (and to the South of) the junction of Wessex Way (A338) and Castle Lane (A3060).

MANGAPPS RAILWAY MUSEUM

Address: Southminster Road, Burnham-on-Crouch, Essex   CM0 8QQ
Telephone Nº: (01621) 784898
Year Formed: 1989
Location of Line: Mangapps Farm
Length of Line: ¾ mile

Nº of Steam Locos: 6
Nº of Other Locos: 10
Nº of Members: –
Annual Membership Fee: –
Approx Nº of Visitors P.A.: 20,000
Gauge: Standard
Web site: www.mangapps.co.uk

GENERAL INFORMATION

Nearest Mainline Station: Burnham-on-Crouch (1 mile)
Nearest Bus Station: –
Car Parking: Ample free parking at site
Coach Parking: Ample free parking at site
Souvenir Shop(s): Yes
Food & Drinks: Yes – drinks and snacks only

SPECIAL INFORMATION

The Railway endeavours to recreate the atmosphere of an East Anglian light railway. It also includes an extensive museum with an emphasis on East Anglian items and signalling.

OPERATING INFORMATION

Opening Times: Closed during January and November, then open every weekend and Bank Holiday (except over Christmas). Open from 11.30am to 5.00pm. Santa Specials run during weekends in December. Please contact the railway for further details.
Steam Working: Bank Holiday Sundays and Mondays plus certain other dates. Diesel at other times. Please contact the railway for further details.
Prices: Adult – Steam £8.00;   Diesel £7.00
Child – Steam £3.50;   Diesel £3.00
Senior Citizen – Steam £7.00; Diesel £6.00
Note: Prices for special events may differ.

Detailed Directions by Car:
From South & West: From M25 take either the A12 or A127 and then the A130 to Rettendon Turnpike and then follow signs to Burnham; From North: From A12 take A414 to Oak Corner then follow signs to Burnham.

MID-HANTS RAILWAY (WATERCRESS LINE)

Address: The Railway Station, Alresford, Hampshire   SO24 9JG
Telephone Nº: (01962) 733810 General enquiries; (01962) 734866 Timetable
Year Formed: 1977
Location of Line: Alresford to Alton
Length of Line: 10 miles

Nº of Steam Locos: 16
Nº of Other Locos: 8
Nº of Members: 3,500
Annual Membership Fee: Adult £20.00
Approx Nº of Visitors P.A.: 150,000
Gauge: Standard
Web Site: www.watercressline.co.uk

Photo courtesy of David Warwick

GENERAL INFORMATION

Nearest Mainline Station: Alton (adjacent) or Winchester (7 miles)
Nearest Bus Station: Winchester or Alton
Car Parking: Pay and display at Alton and Alresford Stations (Alresford free on Sundays & Bank Holidays)
Coach Parking: By arrangement at Alresford Station
Souvenir Shop(s): At Alresford, Ropley & Alton
Food & Drinks: Yes – Buffet on most trains. 'West Country' buffet at Alresford

SPECIAL INFORMATION

The railway runs through four fully restored stations and has a Loco yard and picnic area at Ropley.

OPERATING INFORMATION

Opening Times: Weekends and Bank Holidays from January to October plus Tuesday to Thursday from May to the end of July. Daily during the School holidays. Santa Specials run at weekends and on other dates in December.
Steam Working: All operating days although a Steam/DMU combination is sometimes in service.
Prices: Adult £12.00
Child (ages 2 to 16) £6.00
Family £30.00 (2 adults + 2 children)
A discount is available for pre-booked parties of 15 or more people. Write or call for a booking form.

Detailed Directions by Car:
From the East: Take the M25 then A3 and A31 to Alton; From the West: Exit the M3 at Junction 9 and take the A31 to Alresford Station.

MILTON KEYNES LIGHT RAILWAY

Address: Caldecotte Arms, Bletcham Way, Milton Keynes MK7 8HP	**Nº of Steam Locos:** 4
Telephone Nº: (01908) 503889 (Chairman)	**Nº of Other Locos:** 2
Year Formed: 1972	**Nº of Members:** 40
Location of Line: Caldecotte Arms, Milton Keynes	**Annual Membership Fee:** £35.00 Adult
Length of Line: 280 metres (raised track)	**Approx Nº of Visitors P.A.:** 2,000
	Gauge: 3½ inches and 5 inches
	Web site: www.mklightrailway.co.uk

GENERAL INFORMATION

Nearest Mainline Station: Milton Keynes Central (3 miles)
Nearest Bus Station: Milton Keynes Central
Car Parking: Available on site
Coach Parking: Available on site
Souvenir Shop(s): None
Food & Drinks: Available at the Caldecotte Arms

SPECIAL INFORMATION

The MK Light Railway is operated by members of the Milton Keynes Model Engineering Society. The Society recently received planning permission to lay a ground level track for 5 inch and 7¼ inch gauge engines. The first stage is under construction and will be 300 metres in length. Further extensions are planned to take the line to 1¼ miles in length.

OPERATING INFORMATION

Opening Times: Every Sunday from March to September from 12.00pm to 4.00pm. Open the first Sunday of the month from October through to February subject to weather conditions, also from 12.00pm to 4.00pm.
Steam Working: Most operating days.
Prices: £1.00 per person (twice round the track)

Detailed Directions by Car:
From the North: Exit the M1 at Junction 13 and take the A421 into Milton Keynes. At the 2nd roundabout, turn left into Tongwell Street (A4146). Continue along this road then turn right at the 2nd roundabout into Bletcham Way, go straight on at the next roundabout and turn back on yourself at the following roundabout and the Caldecotte Arms is on the left and easy to see with a replica Windmill as part of the building!
From the South: Exit the M1 at Junction 9 and follow the A5 for approximately 15 miles into Milton Keynes. Turn off the A5 onto the A4146 Bletcham Way and the Caldecotte Arms is on the left after a short distance.

MOORS VALLEY RAILWAY

Address: Moors Valley Country Park, Horton Road, Ashley Heath, Nr. Ringwood, Hants. BH24 2ET **Telephone Nº:** (01425) 471415 **Year Formed:** 1985 **Location of Line:** Moors Valley Country Park	**Length of Line:** 1 mile **Nº of Steam Locos:** 15 **Nº of Other Locos:** 2 **Nº of Members:** – **Approx Nº of Visitors P.A.:** 100,000 **Gauge:** 7¼ inches **Web site:** www.moorsvalleyrailway.co.uk

GENERAL INFORMATION

Nearest Mainline Station: Bournemouth (12 miles)
Nearest Bus Station: Ringwood (3 miles)
Car Parking: Parking charges vary throughout the year. Maximum charge £8.00 per day.
Coach Parking: Charges are applied for parking
Souvenir Shop(s): Yes + Model Railway Shop
Food & Drinks: Yes

SPECIAL INFORMATION

The Moors Valley Railway is a complete small Railway with signalling and 2 signal boxes and also 4 tunnels and 2 level crossings.

OPERATING INFORMATION

Opening Times: Weekends throughout the year. Daily from one week before to one week after Easter, Spring Bank Holiday to mid-September, during School half-term holidays and also from Boxing Day to end of School holidays. Also Santa Specials in December and occasional other openings. Phone the Railways for details.
Steam Working: 10.45am to 5.00pm when open.
Prices: Adult Return £3.00; Adult Single £1.70
Child Return £2.00; Child Single £1.20
Special rates are available for parties of 10 or more.

Detailed Directions by Car:
From All Parts: Moors Valley Country Park is situated on Horton Road which is off the A31 Ferndown to Ringwood road near the junction with the A338 to Bournemouth.

NORTHOLT MODEL RAILWAY CLUB

Address: Northolt Village Community Centre, Ealing Road, Northolt, Middlesex UB5 6AD **Phone N°:** (01753) 652678 (Secretary) **Year Formed:** 1950 **Location of Line:** Northolt, Middlesex **Length of Line:** 680 feet	**N° of Steam Locos:** 10 **N° of Other Locos:** 1 **N° of Members:** 60+ **Approx N° of Visitors P.A.:** 300 **Gauge:** 3½ inches and 5 inches **Web site:** www.northolt-mrc.org.uk

GENERAL INFORMATION

Nearest Mainline Station: Greenford (1 mile)
Nearest Tube Station: Northolt (½ mile)
Car Parking: Street parking only
Coach Parking: None
Food & Drinks: Light refreshments available

SPECIAL INFORMATION

Northolt Model Railway Club was formed in 1950 and has its permanent accommodation situated within the Northolt Village Community Centre. The track, which runs around the Community Centre perimeter, was built between 1962 and 1965.

OPERATING INFORMATION

Opening Times: 2010 dates: 18th April, 16th May, 20th June, 18th July, 15th August, 11th September. Trains run from 2.00pm to 5.00pm.
Steam Working: Every operational day.
Prices: 25p per ride.

Detailed Directions by Car:
Exit the A40 at the Target roundabout and follow signs, heading northwards, for Northolt on the A312 Church Road. Take the third turning on the right (also Church Road) and turn right again at the bottom of the road and the Community Centre and its grounds can be seen on the right hand side. Street parking only is available.

OLD KILN LIGHT RAILWAY

Address: Rural Life Centre, Reeds Road, Tilford, Farnham, Surrey GU10 2DL	**Nº of Steam Locos:** 2
Telephone Nº: (01252) 795571	**Nº of Other Locos:** 10
Year Formed: 1975	**Nº of Members:** 14
Location: 3 miles south of Farnham	**Annual Membership Fee:** £25.00
Length of Line: ¾ mile	**Approx Nº of Visitors P.A.:** 21,000
	Gauge: 2 feet
	Web site: www.oldkilnlightrailway.com

GENERAL INFORMATION

Nearest Mainline Station: Farnham (4 miles)
Nearest Bus Station: Farnham
Car Parking: Free parking available on site
Coach Parking: Free parking available on site
Souvenir Shop(s): Yes
Food & Drinks: Available

SPECIAL INFORMATION

The Railway is part of the Rural Life Centre at Tilford. The Centre contains the biggest country life collection in the South of England with a wide range of attractions. A line extension to ¾ mile has recently been opened.

OPERATING INFORMATION

Opening Times: 2010 dates: The Rural Life Centre is open Wednesday to Sunday and Bank Holidays from 11th March to 31st October 10.00am – 5.00pm. Open Wednesdays and Sundays only during the winter 11.00am – 4.00pm.
Steam Working: Bank Holidays and special events once a month – please check the web site for details. Also for Santa Specials. Diesel at all other times.
Prices: Steam-hauled rides £1.50
   Diesel-hauled rides £1.00

Detailed Directions by Car:
The Rural Life Centre is situated 3 miles south of Farnham. From Farnham take the A287 southwards before turning left at Millbridge crossroads into Reeds Road. The Centre is on the left after about ½ mile, just after the Frensham Garden Centre; From the A3: Turn off at the Hindhead crossroads and head north to Tilford. Pass through Tilford, cross the River Wey then turn left into Reeds Road. The Centre is on the right after ½ mile.

PARADISE WILDLIFE PARK WOODLAND RAILWAY

Address: White Stubbs Lane, Broxbourne   EN10 7QA
Telephone Nº: (01992) 470490
Year Formed: 1981
Location of Line: Paradise Wildlife Park
Length of Line: 300 yards

Nº of Steam Locos: None
Nº of Other Locos: 2
Nº of Members: –
Approx Nº of Visitors P.A.: 25,000
Gauge: 10¼ inches
Web site: www.pwpark.com

GENERAL INFORMATION

Nearest Mainline Station: Broxbourne (2 miles)
Nearest Bus Station: Harlow (6 miles)
Car Parking: Available on site
Coach Parking: Available
Souvenir Shop(s): Yes
Food & Drinks: Available

SPECIAL INFORMATION

A free minibus service is available to take visitors from Broxbourne Railway Station to the Park.

OPERATING INFORMATION

Opening Times: Daily except for Christmas Day. Open from 10.00am to 5.00pm (trains run on request).
Steam Working: None
Prices: Adults £16.00 (Park admission)
Children £11.00 (Park admission)
Concessions £11.00 (Park admission)
Family Ticket £50.00 (Park admission)
Note: Train rides are an extra £1.00 per person

Detailed Directions by Car:
From All Parts: Exit the M25 at Junction 25 and take the A10 Northbound past Cheshunt to Broxbourne. Paradise Wildlife Park is located in Broxbourne Woods and is clearly signposted from the main road.

PINEWOOD MINIATURE RAILWAY

Address: Pinewood Leisure Centre, Old Wokingham Road, Wokingham, Berkshire RG40 3AQ **Phone Nº:** (0118) 989-4516 (Secretary) **Year Formed:** 1984 **Location:** Pinewood Leisure Centre **Length of Line:** 800 metres	**Nº of Steam Locos:** 30 (All owned **Nº of Other Locos:** 10 by Members) **Nº of Members:** Approximately 35 **Annual Membership Fee:** £35.00 **Approx Nº of Visitors P.A.:** 3,000 **Gauge:** 5 inches and 7¼ inches **Web site:** www.pinewoodrailway.co.uk

GENERAL INFORMATION

Nearest Mainline Station: Bracknell
Nearest Bus Station: Bracknell
Car Parking: Available on site
Coach Parking: Available by arrangement
Souvenir Shop(s): None
Food & Drinks: Tea/Coffee making facilities only

SPECIAL INFORMATION

The Pinewood Miniature Railway runs through attractive woodlands backing on to a Leisure Centre.

OPERATING INFORMATION

Opening Times: Year-round work sessions on Sunday mornings and all day on Wednesdays.
Steam Working: Members Steam Up on 1st Sunday of the month. Public running on the 3rd Sunday in the month from April to October. Santa Specials on some dates in December (pre-booking is advised). Private Parties can sometimes be catered for by prior arrangement.
Prices: 80p per ride

Detailed Directions by Car:
From the M3 or the A30 take the A322 towards Bracknell. Once on the A322, keep in the left hand lane to the first major roundabout then take the first exit onto the B3430 towards Wokingham along Nine Mile Ride. Cross the next roundabout (A3095) and continue on the B3430 passing the Golden Retriever pub and the Crematorium. Go straight on at the next mini-roundabout then turn right at the following roundabout into Old Wokingham Road. The Pinewood Leisure Centre is on the left after approximately 100 metres.

READING SOCIETY OF MODEL ENGINEERS

Address: Prospect Park, Bath Road, Reading, Berkshire RG30 2BQ
Telephone Nº: None
Year Formed: 1909 (line since 1975)
Location of Line: Prospect Park, Reading
Length of Line: Two lines, one of 1,050 feet and one of 1,300 feet

Nº of Steam Locos: Approximately 100
Nº of Other Locos: Approximately 20
Nº of Members: 130
Annual Membership Fee: £36.00
Approx Nº of Visitors P.A.: 7,500
Gauge: 2½ inches, 3½ inches, 5 inches and 7¼ inches
Web site: www.prospectparkrailway.co.uk

GENERAL INFORMATION

Nearest Mainline Station: Reading (2 miles)
Nearest Bus Station: Reading Station (2 miles)
Car Parking: Available on site
Coach Parking: Available by prior arrangement
Souvenir Shop(s): None
Food & Drinks: Available

SPECIAL INFORMATION

The Reading SME has been using the current site for more than 40 years and it now boasts a well equipped club house and useful workshop facilities.

OPERATING INFORMATION

Opening Times: The first Sunday of the month throughout the year plus some Bank Holiday Sundays. Trains run from 1.00pm to 5.00pm (until 4.00pm during the Winter months).
Steam Working: All operating days
Prices: 50p per ride

Detailed Directions by Car:
Exit the M4 at Junction 12 and take the A4 Bath Road towards Reading. Continue on this road for approximately 2¼ miles. Prospect Park is on the left, continue along Bath Road almost to the end of Prospect Park and the entrance to the car park for the railway is on the left about 100 metres before the traffic lights.

Romney, Hythe & Dymchurch Railway

Address: New Romney Station, New Romney, Kent TN28 8PL
Telephone Nº: (01797) 362353
Year Formed: 1927
Location of Line: Approximately 5 miles west of Folkestone
Length of Line: 13½ miles

Nº of Steam Locos: 11
Nº of Other Locos: 5
Nº of Members: 2,500
Annual Membership Fee: Supporters association – Adult £19.00; Junior £7.50
Approx Nº of Visitors P.A.: 160,000
Gauge: 15 inches
Web site: www.rhdr.org.uk

GENERAL INFORMATION

Nearest Mainline Station: Folkestone Central (5 miles) or Rye
Nearest Bus Station: Folkestone (then take bus to Hythe)
Car Parking: Free parking at all major stations
Coach Parking: At New Romney & Dungeness
Souvenir Shop(s): Yes – 4 at various stations
Food & Drinks: 2 Cafes serving food and drinks

SPECIAL INFORMATION

Opened in 1927 as 'The World's Smallest Public Railway'. Now the only 15" gauge tourist main line railway in the world. Double track, 6 stations.

OPERATING INFORMATION

Opening Times: 2010 dates: A daily service runs from 27th March to 7th November. Open at weekends in February, March and for Santa Specials during December. Also open daily during School half-terms.
Steam Working: All operational days.
Prices: Depend on length of journey. Maximum fares:

Adult £14.00
Child £7.00
Family £38.00 (2 adults + 2 children)

Detailed Directions by Car:
Exit the M20 at Junction 11 then follow signs to Hythe and the brown tourist signs for the railway. Alternatively, Take the A259 to New Romney and follow the brown tourist signs for the railway.

ROXBOURNE PARK MINIATURE RAILWAY

Address: Roxbourne Park,
Field End Road, Eastcote, Middlesex
Telephone Nº: None
Year Formed: 1936
Location of Line: Roxbourne Park
Length of Line: 2,200 feet

Nº of Steam Locos: Members locos only
Nº of Other Locos: Members locos only
Nº of Members: Approximately 100
Approx Nº of Visitors P.A.: 2,500
Gauge: 3½ inches, 5 inches & 7¼ inches
Web site: www.hwsme.org.uk

GENERAL INFORMATION

Nearest Tube Station: Eastcote (½ mile)
Nearest Bus Station: –
Car Parking: Available on site
Coach Parking: None
Food & Drinks: None

SPECIAL INFORMATION

The railway is operated by members of the Harrow & Wembley Society of Model Engineers which has been running passenger services on the current track in Roxbourne Park since 1979.

OPERATING INFORMATION

Opening Times: 2010 dates: Every Sunday from 28th March to 31st October inclusive. Trains run from 2.30pm to 5.00pm. Santa trains also operate on 12th December from 1.00pm to 4.00pm.
Steam Working: Every operating day.
Prices: 50p per ride.

Detailed Directions by Car:
Exit the M40 at Target roundabout and travel into Northolt Village on the A312. Turn left into Eastcote Lane North after the traffic lights just after Northolt Station and continue along this road. Eastcote Lane becomes Field End Road and Roxbourne Park is a little further on opposite Venue '5' (formerly The Clay Pigeon Public House).

ROYAL VICTORIA RAILWAY

Address: Royal Victoria Country Park, Netley, Southampton   SO31 5GA
Telephone Nº: (023) 8045-6246
Year Formed: 1995
Location of Line: Netley
Length of Line: 1 mile

Nº of Steam Locos: 10
Nº of Other Locos: 9
Nº of Members: None
Approx Nº of Visitors P.A.: Not known
Gauge: 10¼ inches
Web site: www.royalvictoriarailway.co.uk

GENERAL INFORMATION

Nearest Mainline Station: Netley
Nearest Bus Station: Southampton
Car Parking: Available on site – £1.20 fee
Coach Parking: Free parking available on site
Souvenir Shop(s): Yes
Food & Drinks: Yes

SPECIAL INFORMATION

The railway runs through the grounds of an old Victorian hospital and has good views of the Solent and the Isle of Wight. The Park covers 200 acres including woodland, grassland, beaches and picnic sites.

OPERATING INFORMATION

Opening Times: Weekends throughout the year and daily during school holidays. Trains run from 11.00am to 4.30pm. The railway also opens by appointment for larger parties.
Steam Working: On special event days only. Please phone for further details.
Prices: Adult Return £1.75
             Child Return £1.25
Note: Special rates are available for groups of 10 or more when pre-booked. Under-2s travel free.

Detailed Directions by Car:
From All Parts: Exit the M27 at Junction 8 and follow the Brown Tourist signs for the Royal Victoria Country Park. You will reach the Park after approximately 3 miles.

RUISLIP LIDO RAILWAY

Address: Reservoir Road, Ruislip, Middlesex HA4 7TY	**N⁰ of Steam Locos**: 1
Telephone N⁰: (01895) 622595	**N⁰ of Other Locos**: 5
Year Formed: 1979	**N⁰ of Members**: 155
Location of Line: Trains travel from Ruislip Lido to Woody Bay	**Annual Membership Fee**: £15.00
	Approx N⁰ of Visitors P.A.: 60,000
	Gauge: 12 inches
Length of Line: 1¼ miles	**Web site**: www.ruisliplidorailway.org

Photo courtesy of Peter Musgrave

GENERAL INFORMATION

Nearest Mainline Station: West Ruislip (2 miles)
Nearest Bus Station: Ruislip Underground Station
Car Parking: Free parking available at the Lido
Coach Parking: Free parking available at the Lido
Souvenir Shop(s): Yes
Food & Drinks: A Beach Cafe is open on weekends and Bank Holidays. A Pub/Restaurant is open daily.

SPECIAL INFORMATION

The steam locomotive, 'Mad Bess' used by Ruislip Lido Railway was actually built by the members over a 12 year period!

OPERATING INFORMATION

Opening Times: Weekends from mid-February to the end of May and also daily during school holidays. Also open on weekends from September to November and on Sundays in December.
Steam Working: Sundays and Bank Holidays from July to the end of September and also Santa Specials.
Prices: Adult Return £2.50 (Single fare £2.00)
Child Return £2.00 (Single fare £1.50)
Family Return £7.00 (Single fare £6.00)
(2 adults + 2 children)

Detailed Directions by Car:
From All Parts: Follow the signs from the A40 and take the A4180 through Ruislip before turning left onto the B469.

Saffron Walden & District s.m.e.

Correspondence: The Secretary, 'Baltana', London Road, Barkway, Royston SG8 8EY	**Length of Line**: 1,500 feet
	Nº of Steam Locos: 14
	Nº of Other Locos: 8
Telephone Nº: (01763) 848228	**Nº of Members**: 50
Year Formed: 1980	**Approx Nº of Visitors P.A.**: 2,500
Location of Line: Audley End Miniature Railway	**Gauge**: 3½ inches, 5 inches & 7¼ inches
	Web site: www.swdsme.org.uk

GENERAL INFORMATION

Nearest Mainline Station: Audley End (1 mile)
Nearest Bus Station: Saffron Walden (1 mile)
Car Parking: Available on site
Coach Parking: Available on site
Souvenir Shop(s): Yes
Food & Drinks: Snacks available

SPECIAL INFORMATION

The Saffron Walden & District Society of Model Engineers uses a track at Audley End Steam Railway, Lord Braybrooke's private 10¼ inch railway situated just next to Audley End House, an English Heritage site.

OPERATING INFORMATION

Opening Times: Most Saturdays and Sundays from April to October inclusive. Trains run from 2.00pm to 5.00pm.
Steam Working: Most operating days.
Prices: £1.00 per ride (A Multi-ticket is £3.00)

Detailed Directions by Car:
Exit the M11 at Junction 10 if southbound or Junction 9 if northbound and follow the signs for Audley End House. The railway is situated just across the road from Audley End House.

SOUTHALL RAILWAY CENTRE

Address: Armstrong Way, Southall, Middlesex	**N° of Steam Locos**: 5
Telephone N°: (020) 8574-1529	**N° of Other Locos**: 3
Year Formed: 1976	**N° of Members**: 210
Location of Line: Southall, Middlesex	**Annual Membership Fee**: £15.00
Length of Line: Demonstration line only	**Approx N° of Visitors P.A.**: 3,000
	Gauge: Standard
	Web site: www.gwrpg.co.uk

GENERAL INFORMATION

Nearest Mainline Station: Southall (½ mile)
Nearest Bus Station: Hounslow (2 miles)
Car Parking: Ample parking available on site
Coach Parking: Available on site
Souvenir Shop(s): Yes
Food & Drinks: Yes

SPECIAL INFORMATION

The Southall Railway Centre is operated by members of the G.W.R. Preservation Group Ltd.

OPERATING INFORMATION

At the time of going to press, the GWR Preservation Group were still engaged in negotiations with Network Rail to relocate their activities to a different area of the Southall site. Please check their web site shown above for the latest information about the relocation and possible 2010 opening dates.

Detailed Directions by Car:
Exit the M4 at Junction 3 and follow the A312 northwards. Turn right at the roundabout onto the A4020 Uxbridge Road. Continue along the A4020 through Southall passing the Park on the right hand side then turn right into Windmill Lane just after passing beneath the railway line. From Windmill Lane turn into Armstrong Way (industrial estate) and pass through the security point, following the road to the very end (Collett Way), turning right and then immediately left into the road leading up to Southall Railway Centre on the right hand side.

SOUTH DOWNS LIGHT RAILWAY

Address: South Downs Light Railway, Stopham Road, Pulborough RH20 1DS
Telephone Nº: (07711) 717470
Year Formed: 1999
Location: Pulborough Garden Centre
Length of Line: 1 kilometre

Nº of Steam Locos: 10
Nº of Other Locos: 2
Nº of Members: 60
Annual Membership Fee: Adult £20.00
Approx Nº of Visitors P.A.: 15,000
Gauge: 10¼ inches
Web site: www.sdlrs.com

GENERAL INFORMATION

Nearest Mainline Station: Pulborough (½ mile)
Nearest Bus Station: Bus stop just outside Centre
Car Parking: Free parking on site
Coach Parking: Free parking on site
Souvenir Shop(s): Yes
Food & Drinks: Yes – in the Garden Restaurant

SPECIAL INFORMATION

The members of the Society own and operate the largest collection of 10¼ inch gauge scale locomotives in the UK. The Railway is sited in the Wyevale Garden Centre.

OPERATING INFORMATION

Opening Times: Weekends and Bank Holidays from March until September, Wednesdays in August and also Santa Specials at weekends in December. Trains run from 11.00am to 3.30pm.
Steam Working: Most services are steam hauled.
Prices: Adult £1.50
    Child £1.00 (Under-2s travel free of charge)
Note: Supersaver tickets are also available.

Detailed Directions by Car:
From All Parts: The Centre is situated on the A283, ½ mile west of Pulborough. Pulborough itself is on the A29 London to Bognor Regis Road.

Southend Pier Railway

Address: Western Esplanade, Southend-on-Sea SS1 1EE	**Nº of Steam Locos:** None
Telephone Nº: (01702) 618747	**Nº of Other Locos:** 2
Year Formed: 1889	**Nº of Members:** –
Location of Line: Southend seafront	**Approx Nº of Visitors P.A.:** 300,000
Length of Line: 2,180 yards	**Gauge:** 3 feet
	Web site: www.southend.gov.uk/ content.asp?section=583

GENERAL INFORMATION

Nearest Mainline Station: Southend Central (¼ mile)
Nearest Bus Station: Southend (¼ mile)
Car Parking: Available on the seafront
Coach Parking: Available
Souvenir Shop(s): Yes
Food & Drinks: Available

SPECIAL INFORMATION

The railway takes passengers to the end of Southend Pier which, at 1.33 miles, is the longest pleasure pier in the world.

OPERATING INFORMATION

Opening Times: Daily except for Christmas Day. Times vary depending on the season – trains run from 8.30am to 7.00pm during the Summer.
Steam Working: None.
Prices: Adult Return £3.50
Child Return £1.75
Concessionary Return £1.75
Family Return Ticket £8.50

Detailed Directions by Car:
From All Parts: Take the A127 to Southend and follow the brown tourist signs to the Pier.

SPA VALLEY RAILWAY

Address: West Station, Tunbridge Wells, Kent TN2 5QY	**Nº of Steam Locos**: 10
Telephone Nº: (01892) 537715	**Nº of Other Locos**: 9
Year Formed: 1985	**Nº of Members**: Approximately 660
Location of Line: Tunbridge Wells West to Groombridge	**Annual Membership Fee**: £15.00
Length: 5 miles	**Approx Nº of Visitors P.A.**: 30,000
	Gauge: Standard
	Web Site: www.spavalleyrailway.co.uk

Photo courtesy of David Staines

GENERAL INFORMATION

Nearest Mainline Station: Tunbridge Wells Central (½ mile) or Eridge (once the line extension is open)
Nearest Bus Stop: Outside Sainsbury's (100yds)
Car Parking: Available nearby
Coach Parking: Coach station in Montacute Road (150 yards)
Souvenir Shop(s): Yes
Food & Drinks: Yes

SPECIAL INFORMATION

The Railway's Tunbridge Wells Terminus is in a historic and unique L.B. & S.C.R. engine shed. An extension of the line to Groombridge is now open and tickets inclusive of entry to Groombridge Place Manor House and Gardens are available.

OPERATING INFORMATION

Opening Times: 2010 dates: Weekends from 2nd April to 31st October. Some weekdays during School Holidays and also Santa Specials during December. Please contact the railway for further details.
Steam Working: Most services are steam-hauled. Trains run from 10.30am to 5.00pm (11.00am to 3.30pm midweek and during low season).
Prices: Adult Return £9.00
Child Return £4.50
Senior Citizen Return £8.00
Family Return £23.00 (2 adult + 2 child)
Discounts are available for groups of 20 or more.
Fares vary on some special event days.
Fares allow unlimited travel on the day of issue except for special event days.

Detailed Directions by Car:
The Spa Valley Railway is in the southern part of Tunbridge Wells, 100 yards off the A26. Station is adjacent to Sainsbury's and Homebase. Car Parks are nearby in Major Yorks Road, Union House & Linden Close.

STANSTED PARK LIGHT RAILWAY

Address: Stansted House, Rowlands Castle PO9 6DX	**Nº of Steam Locos:** 5
Telephone Nº: (023) 9241-3324	**Nº of Other Locos:** 3
Year Formed: 2005	**Nº of Members:** –
Location: Rowlands Castle, Hampshire	**Approx Nº of Visitors P.A.:** 20,000
Length of Line: ½ mile	**Gauge:** 7¼ inches
	Web site: www.splr.info

GENERAL INFORMATION

Nearest Mainline Station: Rowlands Castle (1¼ miles)
Nearest Bus Station: Hilsea Portsmouth (5 miles)
Car Parking: Available on site
Coach Parking: Available
Souvenir Shop(s): At the Garden Centre
Food & Drinks: Available

SPECIAL INFORMATION

The railway is located within the grounds of Stansted House which stands in 1,800 acres of ancient forest on the South Downs.

OPERATING INFORMATION

Opening Times: Wednesdays, weekends and Bank Holidays throughout the year and daily during the School Holidays. Trains run from 10.00am to 4.00pm.
Steam Working: Most opening days during the Summer, weather permitting.
Prices: Adults £1.50
Children £1.00 (Free for Under-2s)

Detailed Directions by Car:
From All Parts: Exit the A3(M) at Junction 2 and take the B2149 towards Rowlands Castle.

SUMMERFIELDS MINIATURE RAILWAY

Address: Summerfields Farm, Haynes, Bedford MK45 3BH	**N° of Steam Locos**: 8
Telephone N°: (01234) 301867	**N° of Other Locos**: 7
Year Formed: 1948	**N° of Members**: Approximately 180
Location: Off the A600, North of Haynes	**Annual Membership Fee**: £32.00
Length of Line: Approximately ¾ mile	**Approx N° of Visitors P.A.**: 10,000
	Gauge: 7¼ inches
	Web site: www.summerfieldsmr.co.uk

GENERAL INFORMATION

Nearest Mainline Station: Bedford (5½ miles)
Nearest Bus Station: Bedford
Car Parking: Available on site
Coach Parking: Available on site
Souvenir Shop(s): None
Food & Drinks: Available

SPECIAL INFORMATION

Summerfields Miniature Railway is operated by the Bedford Model Engineering Society.

OPERATING INFORMATION

Opening Times: Opening times vary – please phone for details.
Steam Working: On all public running days
Prices: Adult Return £1.50
        Child Return £1.50

Detailed Directions by Car:
From All Parts: The Railway is located by the A600 just to the North of Haynes, 5½ miles South of Bedford and 3½ miles North of Shefford.

Surrey Society of Model Engineers

Address: Mill Lane, Leatherhead, Surrey, KT22 9AA (No post please as the site does not have a letterbox!)	**Nº of Steam Locos:** 10
	Nº of Other Locos: 8
	Nº of Members: 48
Telephone Nº: None	**Approx Nº of Visitors P.A.:** 10,000
Year Formed: 1978	**Gauge:** Both ground and raised level
Location of Line: Mill Lane, Leatherhead	tracks are available covering many gauges
Length of Line: 2,000 feet	**Web site:** www.ssme.co.uk

GENERAL INFORMATION

Nearest Mainline Station: Leatherhead (½ mile)
Nearest Bus Station: Leatherhead (½ mile)
Car Parking: Parking on a grass area is possible when conditions allow
Coach Parking: None
Food & Drinks: Available

OPERATING INFORMATION

Opening Times: Various Bank Holidays on other dates throughout the year. 2010 dates: 1st January, 2nd April, 3rd & 31st May, 27th June, 11th July, 30th August, 12th September and Santa Specials on dates in December. Trains run from 11.00am to 4.00pm. Please contact the railway or check their web site for further details.
Steam Working: All operating days.
Prices: £1.00 per ride
£5.00 multi-ride ticket allows 6 rides
Note: Pre-bookings are required for Santa Specials

Detailed Directions by Car:
The railway is situated near Leatherhead town centre. Mill Lane is across the road from the well signposted Leisure Centre just off the B2122 Waterway Road and just a short walk to the south of Leatherhead Mainline station.

SUTTON HALL RAILWAY

Address: Tabors Farm, Sutton Hall, Shopland Road, near Rochford, Essex SS4 1LQ	**N° of Steam Locos**: 1
	N° of Other Locos: 1
	N° of Members: Approximately 8
Telephone N°: (01702) 334337	**Annual Membership Fee**: £15.00
Year Formed: 1997	**Approx N° of Visitors P.A.**: 3,500
Location of Line: Sutton Hall Farm	**Gauge**: 10¼ inches
Length of Line: Almost 1 mile	**Web site**: None at present

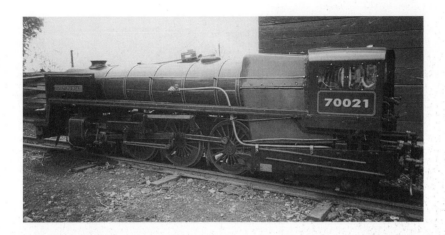

GENERAL INFORMATION

Nearest Mainline Station: Rochford (1½ miles)
Nearest Bus Station: Rochford
Car Parking: Free parking available on site
Coach Parking: Free parking available on site
Souvenir Shop(s): None
Food & Drinks: Drinks and snacks available

SPECIAL INFORMATION

The Railway was bought by C. Tabor in 1985 for use with his Farm Barn Dances. The Sutton Hall Railway Society was formed in 1997 (with C. Tabor as Society President) and now opens the line for public running on some Sundays. The railway is staffed entirely by Volunteer Members of the Society.

OPERATING INFORMATION

Opening Times: Open the 4th Sunday in the month from April until September, 12.00pm to 6.00pm. Specials run on Easter Sunday afternoon, Halloween evening (2.00pm to 10.00pm) and a Santa Special on the afternoon of the 1st Sunday in December.
Steam Working: All operating days.
Prices: Adult Return £2.00
Child Return £1.50

Detailed Directions by Car:
From Southend Airport (A127 Southend to London Main Route & A1159): At the Airport Roundabout (with the McDonalds on the left) go over the railway bridge signposted for Rochford. At the 1st roundabout turn right (Ann Boleyn Pub on the right) into Sutton Road. Continue straight on at the mini-roundabout then when the road forks turn left into Shopland Road signposted for Barling and Great Wakering. Turn right after approximately 400 yards into the long tree-lined road for Sutton Hall Farm.

SWANLEY NEW BARN RAILWAY

Address: Swanley Park, New Barn Road, Swanley BR8 7PW	**Nº of Steam Locos:** 8
Telephone Nº: None	**Nº of Other Locos:** 10
Year Formed: 1986	**Nº of Members:** –
Location of Line: Swanley, Kent	**Approx Nº of Visitors P.A.:** Not known
Length of Line: 900 yards	**Gauge:** 7¼ inches
	Web site: www.snbr.20m.com

GENERAL INFORMATION

Nearest Mainline Station: Swanley (¾ mile)
Nearest Bus Station: Bluewater (9 miles)
Car Parking: Available on site
Coach Parking: Available
Souvenir Shop(s): None
Food & Drinks: Available in the Park

SPECIAL INFORMATION

The railway is located in a Swanley Park which also has play areas, paddling pool, sandpit, boating lake, cafeteria, bouncy castle and battery bikes all set in 60 acres of parkland with free access and parking.

OPERATING INFORMATION

Opening Times: 2010 dates: Weekends and daily during School Holidays from 2nd April to the end of October. Trains run from 11.00am to 5.00pm.
Steam Working: Regular steam working but on an ad hoc basis.
Prices: Adult Return £1.10
Child Return 80p
Family Return £3.00 (2 adults + 2 children)

Detailed Directions by Car:
From All Parts: Exit the M25 at Junction 3 and follow signs for Swanley. Go straight on at the first roundabout then turn right at the second roundabout. Continue straight on at the next roundabout then turn left at the next crossroads into New Barn Road. The Park is on the left side of the road.

THAMES DITTON MINIATURE RAILWAY

Address: Willowbank, Claygate Lane, Thames Ditton, Surrey KT7 0LE	**Nº of Steam Locos**: 30+
Telephone Nº: (020) 8398 3985	**Nº of Other Locos**: 10+
Year Formed: 1936	**Nº of Members**: Approximately 200
Location of Line: Thames Ditton	**Approx Nº of Visitors P.A.**: 15,000
Length of Line: ½ mile	**Gauge**: 3½ inches, 5 inches & 7¼ inches
	Web site: www.malden-dsme.co.uk

GENERAL INFORMATION

Nearest Mainline Station: Thames Ditton (½ mile)
Nearest Bus Station: Thames Ditton
Car Parking: Street parking only
Coach Parking: None
Souvenir Shop(s): Yes
Food & Drinks: Available from 2.30pm onwards

SPECIAL INFORMATION

The railway is operated by Malden and District Society of Model Engineers, is well known locally and is referred to as the Thames Ditton Miniature Railway. The Society operates two tracks at the site – a ground level railway is for larger trains and an elevated railway is for the smaller scale trains. Both are used for passenger hauling services.

OPERATING INFORMATION

Opening Times: Open on Easter Sunday and Monday then the first Sunday of each month and every Bank Holiday Sunday and Monday until the first Sunday in October. Trains run from 2.00pm to 5.30pm though the site is open from 1.00pm onwards. Also open during dates in December for pre-booked Santa Specials – please check the web site for further details.
Steam Working: Every operating day.
Prices: Single ride tickets £2.00
Unlimited ride tickets £5.00
Family tickets £18.00
Note: Prices are correct at the time of publication.

Detailed Directions by Car:
Claygate Lane is located just off the A307 Esher to Kingston road about half a mile to the East of the junction between the A307 and A309. If travelling from the East, Claygate Lane is the turning on the left immediately before the railway bridge. If travelling from the West, Claygate Lane is immediately after the second railway bridge though there is unfortunately, no right turn allowed from this direction.

TONBRIDGE MODEL ENGINEERING SOCIETY

Address: The Slade, Castle Grounds, Tonbridge, Kent TN9 1HR	**N° of Steam Locos:** 40
Telephone N°: (01892) 538415	**N° of Other Locos:** 1
Year Formed: 1944	**N° of Members:** Approximately 100
Location: Castle Grounds, Tonbridge	**Approx N° of Visitors P.A.:** 14,000
Length of Line: ¼ mile	**Gauge:** 3½ inches and 5 inches
	Web site: www.tmes.pwp.blueyonder.co.uk

GENERAL INFORMATION

Nearest Mainline Station: Tonbridge (1 mile)
Nearest Bus Station: Tonbridge (1 mile)
Car Parking: Available on site
Coach Parking: None
Food & Drinks: Available

SPECIAL INFORMATION

The Society has run a track at the present site since 1951 and since then facilities have been extended to include a steaming bay and turntable, passenger trollies, refreshment facilities and meeting room, store, and a well appointed workshop.

OPERATING INFORMATION

Opening Times: Saturday and Sunday afternoons throughout the Summer, weather permitting. Please contact the railway for further information.
Steam Working: Every operating day.
Prices: Free of charge but donations are accepted.

Detailed Directions by Car:
Exit the A21 Tonbridge Bypass at the junction signposted for Tonbridge South. Drive up the High Street, cross over the River Medway and turn left by the sign for the Swimming Pool. Follow the road round, turn left at Slade School and the car park for the railway is directly ahead.

Vanstone Park Miniature Railway

Address: Vanstone Park Garden Centre, Hitchin Road, near Codicote, Hertfordshire SG4 8TH	**N⁰ of Steam Locos:** None
Telephone N⁰: (01438) 820412	**N⁰ of Other Locos:** 4
Year Formed: 1986	**N⁰ of Members:** None
Location: Vanstone Park Garden Centre	**Approx N⁰ of Visitors P.A.:** Not known
Length of Line: 600 yards	**Gauge:** 10¼ inches
	Web site: www.vanstonerailway.co.uk

Address: Vanstone Park Garden Centre, Hitchin Road, near Codicote, Hertfordshire SG4 8TH
Telephone N⁰: (01438) 820412
Year Formed: 1986
Location: Vanstone Park Garden Centre
Length of Line: 600 yards

N⁰ of Steam Locos: None
N⁰ of Other Locos: 4
N⁰ of Members: None
Approx N⁰ of Visitors P.A.: Not known
Gauge: 10¼ inches
Web site: www.vanstonerailway.co.uk

GENERAL INFORMATION

Nearest Mainline Station: Knebworth
Nearest Bus Station: Hitchin
Car Parking: Available on site
Coach Parking: Available on site
Souvenir Shop(s): Yes
Food & Drinks: Yes

SPECIAL INFORMATION

The Railway runs through the Vanstone Park Garden Centre.

OPERATING INFORMATION

Opening Times: Weekends and Bank Holidays throughout the year, weather permitting. Santa Specials run on weekends during December. Please phone to avoid disappointment. Trains run from 11.00am to 4.30pm
Steam Working: None
Prices: Adult Return £1.60
          Child Return £1.20

Detailed Directions by Car:
From All Parts: Exit the A1(M) at Junction 6 and take the B656. Vanstone Park is just off the B656 one mile to the north of Codicote.

VIABLES MINIATURE RAILWAY

Address: Viables Craft Centre,
The Harrow Way, Basingstoke, RG22 4BJ
Telephone N°: None
Year Formed: 1976 (at current location)
Location of Line: Viables Craft Centre
Length of Line: 1,100 feet

N° of Steam Locos: Members locos only
N° of Other Locos: Members locos only
N° of Members: Approximately 65
Approx N° of Visitors P.A.: Not known
Gauge: 3½ inches and 5 inches
Web site: www.basingstoke-dmes.co.uk

GENERAL INFORMATION

Nearest Mainline Station: Basingstoke (2 miles)
Nearest Bus Station: Basingstoke (2 miles)
Car Parking: Free parking available on site
Coach Parking: Available
Souvenir Shop(s): Various shops at the craft centre
Food & Drinks: None available

SPECIAL INFORMATION

The railway is operated by volunteers from the
Basingstoke & District Model Engineering Society
and the current track at Viables Craft Centre opened
in 1979.

OPERATING INFORMATION

Opening Times: The railway runs on the first
Sunday of the month from April to October
inclusive and also in December, weather permitting.
Also a number of other special events – please check
the railway's web site for further details of these.
Trains run from 11.00am to 4.00pm.
Steam Working: Every operating day.
Prices: £1.00 per ride (two circuits of the track).

Detailed Directions by Car:
Viables Craft Centre can be found on the Southern side of Basingstoke, just minutes travel from the A30 and near
the A339 Alton Road and Junction 6 of the M3. The Centre is well signposted locally and is open throughout the
year with free entrance and car parking.

VOLKS ELECTRIC RAILWAY

Address: Arch 285, Madeira Drive, Brighton BN2 1EN	**N⁰ of Steam Locos:** None
Telephone N⁰: (01273) 292718	**N⁰ of Other Locos:** 7
Year Formed: 1883	**N⁰ of Members:** –
Location of Line: Brighton seafront	**Approx N⁰ of Visitors P.A.:** 250,000
Length of Line: 1 mile	**Gauge:** 2 feet 8½ inches
	Web site: www.whitstablepier.com/volks

GENERAL INFORMATION

Nearest Mainline Station: Brighton (2 miles)
Nearest Bus Station: Brighton Pier (¼ mile)
Car Parking: Available on site
Coach Parking: Available
Souvenir Shop(s): Yes
Food & Drinks: Available

SPECIAL INFORMATION

Opened in 1883, Volk's Electric Railway is the world's oldest operating electric railway. The brainchild of inventor Magnus Volk, the railway runs for just over a mile along Brighton seafront between Aquarium (for Brighton Pier) and Black Rock (for the Marina).

OPERATING INFORMATION

Opening Times: 2010 dates: Daily from 2nd April to 30th September, usually from 10.00am to 5.00pm (later starts on Tuesdays and Fridays).
Steam Working: None
Prices: Adult Return £2.80 (Single £1.80)
　　　　　Child Return £1.40 (Single 90p)
　　　　　Concessionary Return £1.80 (Single £1.10)
　　　　　Family Return £6.40 (Single £3.80)

Detailed Directions by Car:
From All Parts: Take the A23/A27 to Brighton and the railway is located on the seafront adjacent to the Pier.

WATERWORKS RAILWAY

Address: Kew Bridge Steam Museum, Green Dragon Lane, Brentford TW8 0EN **Telephone N°**: (020) 8568-4757 **Year Formed**: 1986 **Location of Line**: Greater London **Length of Line**: Under 1 mile	**N° of Steam Locos**: 1 **N° of Other Locos**: 1 **N° of Members**: 750 **Annual Membership Fee**: £20.00 Adult **Approx N° of Visitors P.A.**: 20,000 **Gauge**: 2 feet **Web site**: www.kbsm.org

GENERAL INFORMATION

Nearest Mainline Station: Kew Bridge (3 minute walk)
Nearest Bus Station: Bus stop across the road – Services 65, 267 and 237
Car Parking: Spaces for 43 cars available on site
Coach Parking: Available on site – book in advance
Souvenir Shop(s): Yes
Food & Drinks: Yes – at weekends only

SPECIAL INFORMATION

The Museum is a former Victorian Pumping Station with a collection of working Steam Pumping Engines. The Railway demonstrates typical water board use of Railways.

OPERATING INFORMATION

Opening Times: 11.00am to 4.00pm, from Tuesday to Sunday inclusive throughout the year (closed on Mondays except for Bank Holidays).
Steam Working: Sundays and Bank Holiday Mondays from April to October and also on other special event days.
Prices: Adult £9.50 (Annual ticket)
Child – Free if accompanied by Adults
Senior Citizen £8.50 (Annual ticket)

Detailed Directions by Car:
From All Parts: Exit the M4 at Junction 2 and follow the A4 to Chiswick Roundabout. Take the exit signposted for Kew Gardens & Brentford. Go straight on at the next two sets of traffic lights following A315 towards Brentford. After 2nd set of lights take the first right for the museum. The museum is next to the tall Victorian tower.

WAT TYLER MINIATURE RAILWAY

Address: Pitsea Hall Lane, Pitsea, Basildon SS16 4UH
Telephone Nº: (01268) 275050
Year Formed: 1988
Location of Line: Basildon, Essex
Length of Line: 1 mile
Web site: www.wattylerminiaturerailway.com

Nº of Steam Locos: None
Nº of Other Locos: 2
Nº of Members: –
Approx Nº of Visitors P.A.: 250,000 visitors to the Park – 20,000 rides
Gauge: 10¼ inches

GENERAL INFORMATION

Nearest Mainline Station: East Pitsea (½ mile)
Nearest Bus Station: Basildon (2 miles)
Car Parking: Available on site
Coach Parking: Available
Souvenir Shop(s): None
Food & Drinks: Available

OPERATING INFORMATION

Opening Times: Weekends throughout the year and daily during School Holidays. Open 11.30am to 4.00pm.
Steam Working: None
Prices: Adult Return £2.50
Child Return £1.50

SPECIAL INFORMATION

The railway is located in the Wat Tyler Country Park close to the site of a 19th Century explosives factory.

Detailed Directions by Car:
From All Parts: Exit the A13 at the Pitsea Flyover and follow signs for Wat Tyler Country Park which is approximately ½ mile on the right.

WELLINGTON COUNTRY PARK RAILWAY

Address: Odiham Road, Riseley, RG7 1SP
Telephone Nº: (0118) 932-6444
Year Formed: 1980
Location of Line: Riseley, Berkshire
Length of Line: 500 yards

Nº of Steam Locos: None
Nº of Other Locos: 1
Nº of Members: –
Approx Nº of Visitors P.A.: Not known
Gauge: 7¼ inches
Web site: www.wellington-country-park.co.uk

GENERAL INFO

Nearest Mainline Station: Mortimer (5 miles)
Nearest Bus Station: Reading (9 miles)
Car Parking: Available on site
Coach Parking: Available
Souvenir Shop(s): Yes
Food & Drinks: Available

SPECIAL INFORMATION

The railway is located within 350 acres of beautiful parklands which surround a 35 acre lake.

OPERATING INFO

Opening Times: 2010 dates: Daily from 13th February to 7th November, 9.30am to 5.30pm.
Steam Working: None
Prices: Adults £6.75
            (Park Admission)
            Children £5.75
            (Park Admission)
            Under-3s are admitted free
            Senior Citizens £6.25
            (Park Admission)
            Family Tickets £22.50
            (2 adult + 2 child)
Note: Train rides are an additional £1.00 each.

Detailed Directions by Car:
From All Parts: Exit the M4 at Junction 11 and take the A33 towards Basingstoke. Turn onto the B3349 at the Riseley roundabout and follow the signs to the Park which is straight off the roundabout.

WILLEN LAKE MINIATURE RAILWAY

Address: South Willen Lake,
Milton Keynes   MK15 0DS
Telephone Nº: (01908) 691620
Year Formed: 1989
Location of Line: Milton Keynes
Length of Line: 600 yards

Nº of Steam Locos: None
Nº of Other Locos: 1
Nº of Members: –
Approx Nº of Visitors P.A.: More than
one million visitors to the Park each year
Gauge: 7¼ inches
Web site: None

GENERAL INFORMATION

Nearest Mainline Station: Milton Keynes Central
(1½ miles)
Nearest Bus Station: Milton Keynes (1½ miles)
Car Parking: Available on site
Coach Parking: Available
Souvenir Shop(s): None
Food & Drinks: Available

OPERATING INFORMATION

Opening Times: Weekends and daily during the
School Holidays from April until the end of
October. Open from 11.00am to 5.00pm.
Steam Working: None
Prices: £1.50 per ride

Detailed Directions by Car:
From All Parts: Exit the M1 at Junction 14 and follow the H6 towards Milton Keynes. The lake is to the left of the
road by the V10 (Brickhill Street).

WOKING MINIATURE RAILWAY

Address: Barrs Lane, Knaphill, Woking, Surrey GU21 2JW **Telephone Nº**: (01483) 720801 **Year Formed**: 1989 **Location of Line**: Knaphill, Surrey **Length of Line**: 1 mile	**Nº of Steam Locos**: 10 **Nº of Other Locos**: 6 **Nº of Members**: 110 **Annual Membership Fee**: £15.00 **Approx Nº of Visitors P.A.**: 20,000 **Gauge**: 7¼ inches **Web site**: www.mizensrailway.co.uk

GENERAL INFORMATION

Nearest Mainline Station: Woking
Nearest Bus Station: Woking
Car Parking: 200 spaces available on site
Coach Parking: Available on site
Souvenir Shop(s): Yes
Food & Drinks: Available on running days

SPECIAL INFORMATION

The Railway is situated in a beautiful location admist 8 acres of woodland. In addition to over a mile of track, the railway has three stations, two signalboxes, a tunnel, a Roundhouse Engine Shed, a level crossing and authentic buildings.

OPERATING INFORMATION

Opening Times: Easter Sunday then every Sunday from May to September. Also Thursdays in August. Trains run from 2.00pm to 5.00pm. See the web site for details of Special Events including Santa Specials in December when pre-booking is essential.
Steam Working: Most operating days
Prices: Adult Return £1.50 – £2.00
Child Return £1.50 – £2.00

Detailed Directions by Car:
From All Parts: Exit the M25 at Junction 11 and follow the A320 to Woking. At the Six Cross Roads Roundabout take the 5th exit towards Knaphill then turn left at the roundabout onto Littlewick Road. Continue along Littlewick Road crossing the roundabout before turning right into Barrs Lane just before Knaphill.